Ministry with the Forgotten: Dement.

"...helps to see that dementia is far more than a medical diagnosis or a stigma. Ken Carder's book helped me to reflect on dementia from the vantage point of faith. Also, my understanding of how to relate to people who happen to be on this journey has greatly increased."
—**Joe Pennel**, retired bishop, The United Methodist Church; professor of the practice of leadership, Vanderbilt University Divinity School, Nashville, TN

"...offers a deeper, theologically and scripturally informed understanding of the dimensions of the mind, thought, memory, individuality, consciousness, Christian love/loving, discipleship, community, salvation, and *imago Dei*. Carder offers spiritual insights into the roles and *gifts* of community and ministry *with* and not just *to* those affected. This book will give great comfort to all struggling with faith and spirituality while grappling with dementia. Moreover, he presents the church with great challenges and opportunities for spiritual growth in its response. Fortunately, Carder has many suggestions... but 'the greatest of these is love.'"
—**Don Wendorf and Lynda Everman**, senior editors, *Dementia-Friendly Worship: A Multifaith Handbook for Chaplains, Clergy, and Faith Communities*

"...comes alongside all who have been wounded through dementia's blows—those diagnosed, families and care partners, healthcare providers, clergy and friends—with the blessed ministry of presence. Through sharing personal struggles as his wife's primary care partner, his deep faith so eloquently expressed, and a rich cadre of references, Bishop Carder reframes one of modern medicine's most feared diagnoses in the language of love. This ministry and this book honors the promises of God who 'never will forget us,' and who marks us by God's unfading image and a dignity implicit to the gift."
—**Daniel C. Potts**, MD, Fellow of the American Academy of Neurology; founder and president, Cognitive Dynamics Foundation; and medical director, Dementia Dynamics, LLC, Tuscaloosa, AL

"...is a lovely, thoughtful book, awakening all of us to what our life in Christ is really like. Who better than Bishop Ken Carder to probe, with such wisdom and eloquence, how we think about dementia and Christian faith?"
—**James C. Howell**, PhD, senior pastor, Myers Park UMC, Charlotte, NC

Kenneth L. Carder

Ministry
with the
Forgotten

Dementia through
a Spiritual Lens

Abingdon Press™

Nashville

MINISTRY WITH THE FORGOTTEN:
Dementia through a Spiritual Lens

Copyright © 2019 by Abingdon Press

ISBN 978-1-5018-8024-7

Scripture quotations are from the New Revised Standard Version (NRSV) Bible, copyright © 1989 National Council of the Churches of Christ in the United States of America. Used by permission. All rights reserved worldwide. http://nrsvbibles.org/

19 20 21 22 23 24 25 26 27 28—10 9 8 7 6 5 4 3 2 1
MANUFACTURED IN THE UNITED STATES OF AMERICA

Dedicated to

Linda Miller Carder
beloved spouse who has taught me
the depth, breadth, and permanence of love

and

Sheri Carder Hood and Sandra Carder Nash
cherished daughters who love their mother
with the love they learned from her

Contents

Contents

Foreword

By Warren Kinghorn

"Love has its speed," remarks the theologian Kosuke Koyama.[1] But it is not the speed of our modern, technological age.

For many in our modern world, there are not enough hours in the day. We "run" errands, "grab" meals, and dread "wasting time." In a market-driven culture that assigns value and status based on production, efficiency, and the appearance of control, our lives become a race to protect ourselves against the terrifying possibility of uselessness. Production, efficiency, and control are the ways that we make sure that like any other commodity, we are "valued."

In the face of this, Koyama wonders why, in the biblical stories, God seems to work so slowly. The people of Israel wandered in the wilderness for *forty years*. The Canaanite woman frantically seeking healing for her demon-possessed daughter initially met in Jesus only wordless silence (Matt 15:22-23). Why does God move so slowly?

Koyama suggests that it is in these times, when God seems to move slowly or not at all, that we learn what it means to live in wilderness. Wilderness is the place where danger and promise coexist. Contrary to what our modern world teaches, we do not grow in biblical faith by avoiding danger. Nor do we grow in biblical faith by pursuing happiness and promise. Rather, biblical faith is rooted where danger and promise encircle us, in the wilderness. In the wilderness, unable to control our own lives, we can only trust. "There is a vast difference," Koyama remarks, "between 'happy-end-religion' and 'trust-end-faith.'"[2]

But a remarkable thing happens in the wilderness. Unable to escape, unable to exert control, "our speed is slowed down until gradually we come to the speed on which we walk—*three miles an hour*."[3] It is a slow, agonizing walk. But then we discover that three miles an hour is also the pace that Jesus walked, and therefore the pace that God walks. In the wilderness, slowed to three miles an hour, we find love. Koyama concludes:

> Love has its speed. It is an inner speed. It is a spiritual speed. It is a different kind of speed from the technological speed to which we are accustomed. It is "slow" yet it is lord over all other speeds since it is the speed of love. It goes on in the depth of our life, whether we notice or not, whether we are currently hit by storm or not, at three miles an hour. It is the speed we walk and therefore it is the speed the love of God walks.[4]

Bishop Kenneth Carder and his wife, Linda, are witnesses to us from the wilderness. In the first pages of this book, Dr. Carder writes of the shock and grief that he and Linda experienced when she began showing early signs of frontotemporal dementia. Over the next several years, as the disease affected her life more and more, Dr. Carder retired from his role as a busy professor at a United Methodist seminary and gave up nearly all of his work as a bishop and scholar to become Linda's full-time caregiver. Ken and Linda found themselves in the wilderness, slowed to three miles an hour and, eventually, nearly to a stop. It was, and is, hard.

But an amazing thing happened when the Carders walked with each other in the wilderness. When they were slowed to the speed of love, God met them. The good news of Jesus opened itself in life-giving, beautiful ways. And in this book, from the wilderness, Bishop Carder testifies to a "trust-end-faith" that the church, and indeed every human, deeply needs to hear.

Modern culture and much of modern Christianity lead us to think that our personhood is constituted by our ability to reason, to act, and to produce. But from the wilderness, we learn that beyond anything we can think, do, or produce, we are known and loved by God. We are held in God's memory even when our own fails us.

Foreword

Modern culture and much of modern Christianity lead us to think that dependence and vulnerability are risks to be avoided at all costs. But from the wilderness, we learn that dependence and vulnerability are at the core of what it means to be human.

Modern culture and much of modern Christianity lead us to think that our lives are constituted by our story as we develop it over time. But from the wilderness, we learn that our lives are constituted by God's story, as God claims us, loves us, and restores us.

Modern culture and much of modern Christianity lead us to think that we find God by focusing our thought on a higher, transcendent realm. But from the wilderness, we learn that the God who became flesh finds us in our bodies and holds us in God's life.

Modern culture and much of modern Christianity lead us to think that being saved and being made holy are rooted in our individual belief and work. But from the wilderness, we learn that God is the one who reconciles us and that we belong to each other in community. God redeems us in community and as community and gives us the gifts that we need for the journey.

Bishop Carder has written a generously wise book that is a gift to the church and a healing resource for people living with dementia and all who walk with them and alongside them. Those who are seeking a book on pastoral care and dementia will find here a wealth of theological insight, practical recommendations, and reflections that are grounded in deeply lived experience.

But this is not simply a book about living with dementia or caregiving for those who live with dementia, nor simply a book about pastoral care. It is rather a testimony from the wilderness, a memoir of "trust-end-faith." It is a book about what it means to be a disciple of Jesus Christ in our modern, technological world. It is a book about what it means to be known and loved by God, full stop. It is a book about what it means for love to endure, when all else fails.

Warren Kinghorn, MD, ThD, is Associate Professor of psychiatry at Duke University Medical Center and the Esther Colliflower Associate Professor of the Practice of Pastoral and Moral Theology at Duke Divinity School in Durham, North Carolina.

Acknowledgments

"Dad, you need to share things you are learning on this journey with others," advised our daughters. My initial response was hesitancy, if not outright resistance. Writing requires focused attention and disciplined actions. Dealing with the daily tasks of caregiving made focus and discipline difficult, and the emotional turmoil inherent in living with dementia compounded the challenges. Additionally, the journey is intensely personal, and I did not want to exploit in any way Linda's reality.

Yet, there emerged a conviction that sharing insights from our experience would be a way of living my baptism and ordination in this painful context. I knew that I could not do it alone. It's impossible to name all those who have provided encouragement, guidance, support, and aid; but I do wish to pay special tribute to several key persons.

First and foremost, I am indebted to Linda for almost six decades of love, encouragement, and support. She has taught me what it means to love generously, justly, unconditionally, and courageously. Among her greatest gifts are our daughters, Sheri Carder Hood and Sandra Carder Nash, who love their mother with the love and devotion they learned from her. They are companions on our mutual journey and provide daily assistance, inspiration, and support. The book could not have been written without their help.

The immense influence and contributions of Norma and Dale Sessions are evident throughout the book. Drawing on their professional backgrounds as a social worker specializing in gerontology and chaplain in long-term care facilities and personal experience living with Alzheimer's disease, their input has been invaluable. As close neighbors and friends, they have become partners on a common journey. Dale's exceptional openness and courage in confronting his Alzheimer's is an inspiration and model for dealing with the disease. Norma's love for Dale and exemplary care teach us all; and I am deeply indebted to her for her professional expertise and input.

Karen Young has contributed significantly to my understanding as well as providing pastoral care to Linda and me. As a Lutheran pastor and hospice chaplain, she brings a wealth of experience and insight to our seminary class and to my own knowledge of pastoral care. I'm grateful to the Heritage at Lowman for hosting the seminary class and to the campus chaplain, Derald Edwards, for his support.

Special thanks to Warren Kinghorn for writing the Foreword and for his foundational essay referenced in the book. As a psychiatrist and theologian, he provides a much-needed perspective on dementia. Michael Stephens and Laurie Vaughen's wise counsel and skillful editing significantly strengthened the manuscript.

I am indebted to Lutheran Theological Southern Seminary for the invitation to teach a class on pastoral care and dementia. The students who have participated in the classes have inspired, challenged, and taught me much. Their insights, questions, and experiences have prodded me to continue my own research and theological reflection. Sandy Leach, Associate Director of the Lineberger Library at the seminary, provided invaluable assistance in identifying resources.

Special thanks to a wonderful team of caregivers—Arlene Cromer, Betty Abney, Myleka Praylow, Vanessa Mayers, and Wilma Abney! They have become family to Linda and me! They model servant ministry and true greatness; and their tender, compassionate, and faithful care of Linda has provided space for me to write.

Finally, the residents and staff at Bethany, the memory care facility at the Heritage at Lowman, have been and continue to be my teachers. Serving among them as volunteer chaplain enriches my life beyond measure. They minister to me more than I minister to them, and I am forever grateful.

Introduction
A Personal Journey

On a cold, rainy November day in 2009, my wife, Linda, and I embarked on a treacherous and unwelcomed journey that altered every area of our lives. We sat holding hands in an office at Duke Medical Center awaiting the results of an extensive neurological and cognitive evaluation.

I had noticed subtle changes in Linda that I attributed simply to our aging—slowness in choosing items from a menu, simple miscalculations in bookkeeping, lack of attentiveness in conversation. We did suspect something more serious than normal aging when she was turned down for driver's license renewal. Yet, we both were in a state of denial.

The dramatic changes were more evident to our daughters who lived in another state and lacked the familiarity of constant interaction. Changes can more easily be rationalized or assimilated when they are part of daily life. But subtle and gradual variations in speech and behavior become more obvious to those who observe them after longer absence. Our daughters knew that more than the normal aging process was at play in their mother.

I knew the report was ominous by the somber look on the faces of the doctor, nurse, and social worker. With gentleness and compassion, the doctor shared the diagnosis: frontotemporal dementia. He explained the disease as affecting the frontal lobe of the brain where executive functioning is controlled. We weren't ready to hear the details. The dreaded "d" word (dementia) was enough now. The tears in the physician's eyes indicated that he knew far more what was ahead for us than we imagined.

We drove home in silence born of fear, numbness, dread, and uncertainty. Yet, a deep sense of compassion surfaced as I took Linda's hand and said, "We're in this together." She began to cry, "Don't tell the girls. I don't want anyone to know." I told her that they knew something was amiss and that they will want to know.

We called our daughters, and they assured us that we will face whatever awaits together. I began to feel a strangely unexpected sense of relief. Now there was an explanation for behaviors that I found embarrassing, irritating, and frustrating. Those were the disease, not Linda. We had a name and a reason. Though my impatience and frustration would continue, patience and compassion would grow from separating disease-caused symptoms from personhood.

Therein marked the beginning of what some call "the long goodbye." Indeed, we have bidden farewell to much that we had assumed and valued. Persistent changes in all aspects of our lives have followed. The disease forced immediate and long-term adjustments in our retirement plans, living environment, finances, and activities.

My vocation changed from full-time professor to caregiver. We moved to be near our daughters. Gradually the disease altered Linda's personality and way of relating. Communication faded. I lost my primary conversation partner. Intimacy took on new meaning and expression. Roles changed. Our daughters became mothers to their mother. I often am more of a parent than a spouse.

Grief became a relentless companion as losses multiplied. A friend whose beloved spouse succumbed to a form of dementia said, "It's like a perpetual funeral." Another remarked, "I feel like a part of me is dying day after day." And a wife said, "The person I miss most is sitting right beside me."

Linda's behaviors and personality changed, common symptoms of frontotemporal disease. Frustration, anger, compulsiveness, irritation, restlessness, combativeness, and inner turmoil increased as time passed. I was bewildered and felt increasingly powerless to relieve her anguish. I constantly prayed for Linda's peace while desperately wanting to hold on to her. I longed for Linda as she used to be while I attempted to love her as she had become.

Activities diminished, and the circle of engagement grew smaller and smaller. Social involvements created tension and sometimes embarrassment as filters weakened. Contacts gradually decreased as shared memories and language receded. Discomfort on the part of some family members and friends resulted in fewer visits and calls. Church had been central to our lives, but participation waned as the ability to maintain focus, attentiveness, and proper decorum lessened.

Six years into the journey, a painful decision was made. Combativeness, wandering, and sleeplessness had escalated. I was at my wit's end! Our daughters expressed concern about my own health. They said, "Dad, we're afraid we will lose you, too! We have to do something!" They saw both their parents' well-being in jeopardy. There followed the most difficult and painful decision I have ever made.

Ensuring safety and providing adequate care required that Linda be admitted to the memory care facility in the continuing care retirement community where we lived. For the first time in fifty-five years of marriage, we would be living separately. I felt terrible! Was I abandoning her? The drive across the street to the facility felt like a funeral procession!

Linda was oblivious to where she was being taken, except we had told her she was going to a place that would help her. As we exited the car, I saw the frightened look in her eyes. I took her by the hand and escorted her into the lobby. There we were met by the staff. Linda's words as our daughters and I placed her into hands of staff were "I'm scared!" My heart broke! And those words and images haunt me to this day!

Eighteen agonizing months followed as adjustment to institutional care proceeded and the disease progressed. I visited her two or three times each day, assisting with feeding and personal care. As an introvert who valued privacy, Linda found it difficult accommodating to communal living. Her exceptional modesty resulted in severe resistance to being bathed by staff. She lost more than twenty pounds and her confusion increased.

Linda gradually forgot how to feed herself and her walking became unsteady. The disease moved into the severe stage. Full-time nursing care was the next step, either in the skilled healthcare building or at home with around-the-clock help. After medical evaluation, it was determined that the time for hospice care had arrived. "How much time do we have?" I asked. The nurse practitioner responded, "That's impossible to predict; but given the current rate of decline, I think within six months to a year."

We made the decision to return Linda to our home with full-time assistance. New adjustments followed. Now, strangers would always be in our house. Maintaining reliable, trustworthy, and compatible caregivers was a persistent challenge. After about six months, however, a quality and consistent team of caregivers was in place. They became part of the family.

With the individualized care in a quiet home environment, Linda's physical condition improved. She regained and surpassed her normal weight. Frequent agitation and combativeness continued, but having her nearby made possible more moments of deep connection and joy. The six months passed, and then the year. Slowly, she forgot how to walk and required total assistance for personal care. Her recognition of family members receded and her moments of connection decreased.

Almost three years have passed since she returned to our home, and the journey continues toward her final peace. In the words of the poet William Blake, we "kiss the joy as it flies by" and cherish a fleeting smile or glimmer of recognition.

Prevalence of Dementia

The same day that Linda and I received the dreaded diagnosis, approximately eleven hundred additional people received similar news. According to the 2019 Alzheimer's Association report, 5.8 million people have Alzheimer's or another form of dementia.[1] The following statistics indicate the prevalence of the diseases:[2]

- One in 10 people (10 percent of the US population) age 65 and older has Alzheimer's disease, the most common cause of dementia.

- The number of Americans living with Alzheimer's disease (5.8 million) is projected to rise to nearly 14 million—more than double—by the year 2050.

- Alzheimer's disease is the sixth leading cause of death in the United States.

- Every 65 seconds someone in the US develops the disease.

- The percentage of people with Alzheimer's disease increases with age: 3 percent of people age 65 to 74, 17 percent age 75 to 84, 32 percent age 85 and older.

- Almost two-thirds of Americans with Alzheimer's disease are women.

- Between 2018 and 2025, the number of people with Alzheimer's disease is expected to increase by at least 13 percent.

- An estimated one-third of people 70 and older have a form of dementia when they die.

- Neurocognitive diseases are the sixth leading cause of death, more than breast cancer and prostate cancer combined.

- Between 2000 and 2015, deaths by heart disease decreased by 11 percent while deaths from Alzheimer's disease *increased* by 123 percent.

- More than 18.5 billion hours of informal, unpaid care were provided by dementia caregivers in 2018, a contribution to the nation valued at nearly $234 billion.

- Dementia diseases are estimated to cost Americans $290 billion in health care, long-term care, and hospice in 2019, and by 2050 the amount could increase to $1.1 trillion.

These ominous statistics do not tell the full story. The disorders that cause dementia are underreported and many go undiagnosed. Furthermore, the statistics do not measure the extensive emotional, physical, financial, and relational impact on family members and loved ones of the people with the diseases. Nor does the data identify the spiritual, theological, and ecclesial implications and impact the diseases have on individuals, families, and congregations.

A Theological/Pastoral Journey

Dementia is viewed primarily through medical lenses as a brain disease consisting of behavioral and cognitive symptoms. Understanding the nature, causes, symptoms, and effects of neurocognitive diseases is important. Yet, human beings cannot be reduced to a constellation of symptoms nor defined and valued by their cognitive and physical capacities. We are more than our symptoms and capacities!

The changes and challenges inherent in dementia have theological and spiritual components. Theology provides a needed broader lens and offers needed resources for those who cope with dementia. But dementia can become a crisis of faith for those living with the disease, the patient, the caregivers, and the loved ones.

My personal journey continues to challenge my theological understandings and push me out of my theological/doctrinal and vocational comfort zones. At the same time, my personal faith and vocational calling in baptism and ordination shape my perspective, motivation, and actions as I live with and minister among people enduring cognitive impairments.

Where is God on this treacherous and uncertain journey with dementia? How does one live out a vocational calling in such circumstances? What is the essence of personhood? Is the one you have loved still there when personality and cognitive changes seem to create a different person? What if the person forgets God? Can one be a Christian disciple when she/he has forgotten Jesus? What does it mean to be part of the church when one can no longer participate? What is the role of the church in relationship to those affected by dementia diseases? What finally endures when cognitive capacities are lost? What does salvation/wholeness really mean? How can one hope when loss is a constant companion?

These are among the questions I continue to raise, and experience confirms that I am not alone in these questions. I've spent my adult life proclaiming, interpreting, and teaching basic Christian doctrines and religious practices. Considering those affirmations and practices while living, worshipping, and serving among people with dementia is a profound theological and pastoral transformation. Abstract doctrines, pious platitudes, and superficial reassurances simply don't work! The whole experience cracks open the façade of theological propositions and exposes the harsh realities and messiness in which trustworthy theology emerges.

Linda's diagnosis represented another vocational crossroads. How do I live out my baptism and ordination in such a context? It wasn't the first time that unexpected health problems resulted in new contexts for my ministry. Cardiac bypass surgery and a subsequent heart attack in 2002 resulted in my retirement from the active episcopacy and precipitated a move into a new arena: teaching prospective pastors and church leaders. Serving on the faculty of Duke Divinity School was an unparalleled privilege. I relished being part of an environment where the emphasis is on the intellect and theological reflection. Students and faculty are evaluated on how well they think and communicate.

Now circumstances meant a calling among a very different population. Caregiving was to become my primary vocation. Fulfilling my new calling required learning all I could about the diseases that cause dementia and how best to care for those directly affected by them. I immersed myself in relevant literature, attended seminars and workshops, participated in support groups, and talked with experts and others traveling a similar road.

I was invited to serve as chaplain at Bethany, the memory care facility where Linda spent eighteen months. There I continue to lead worship and Bible study and provide pastoral care for approximately forty residents and their families, plus staff. The residents and those who care for them are profound means of grace and they persistently inform my theological understanding, vocational calling, and Christian discipleship.

Another avenue of ministry has been the development and teaching of a seminary class focusing on pastoral care with people affected by dementia diseases. This book is the outgrowth of the class and experiences with family members and parishioners who live with dementia. It is also an expression of my sense of calling to help others who travel a similar journey.

Overview

This book is based on the conviction that pastoral theology and ministry provide an important lens through which to view people with dementia and much needed resources for living with the diseases. While valuing the resources and tools of medical science and technology, this book offers a complementary perspective and approach to that of medicine and psychology.

First, a brief word about the title. *Ministry* encompasses relationships within and by the church, laity and clergy, directed toward mutual growth toward God's vision for humanity. As used in this volume, it is not to be understood as primarily programmatic or the prerogative of ordained clergy. Additionally, the emphasis is ministry *with* rather than ministry *to* the forgotten. Persons with dementia are participants in, rather than objects of, the church's ministry.

Chapter 1 provides an overview of the current *medical* information related to dementia diseases, including the causes, symptoms, effects, and possible treatments. The brain is a complex and mysterious organ, and "the mind" is more encompassing than cognitive recall; dementia diseases affect behavior, language, and bodily functioning as well as "thinking." Clarifying the medical lens is foundational for broadening the lenses beyond the medical.

Chapter 2 builds upon the medical foundation by focusing on *memory*. A prominent symptom of forms of dementia is "memory loss." Yet, memory is more than cognitive recall, and it plays a significant role in human identity, intra- and interpersonal relationships, and spiritual/theological reflection and practices.

Chapter 3 turns the spotlight on dementia as a *theological* challenge and opportunity. Much of religion emphasizes cognitive reflection and abstractions as well as practices requiring intellectual understanding and prescribed behaviors. Dementia diseases strip away intellectual and language capacities and remove filters controlling behavior. Can people who forget God know God? What if all "beliefs" are erased? What is the church's role and mission when more and more members of the congregation live with dementia disease?

What does *God* have to do with dementia? That is the question addressed in Chapter 4. Creation includes chaos, and dementia diseases reflect a form of chaos, bondage, and exile. The Bible and Christian tradition speak of God working in creation, liberating those in bondage, and entering exile. The nature and action of God offer healing and hope for people affected by dementia diseases.

At the heart of the Christian faith and tradition is *incarnation*. Chapter 5 reflects on the implications of God entering the totality of human experience in Jesus the Christ, including human vulnerability and weakness. Incarnation also implies that God has chosen human personhood as a vehicle of divine presence and action, regardless of personal capacities.

Chapter 6 gives attention to the meaning of *personhood* from a Judeo-Christian perspective. In a culture influenced by the Cartesian dictum "I think, therefore I am," cognitive impairment challenges what it means to be a person of worth and dignity. Christian anthropology provides an alternative to an anthropology heavily weighted on intellect, individualism, and personal capacities.

Chapter 7 considers *salvation* in the light of lost intellectual, relational, linguistic, and behavioral capacities. What does salvation mean when intellectual beliefs, verbal affirmations, ethical decisions, and chosen actions are beyond the abilities of people with debilitating brain diseases? What role does community play in salvation?

Can people who have forgotten who Jesus is be disciples of Jesus? *Discipleship* is popularly defined in terms of prescribed beliefs and practices. Chapter 8 considers the meaning and practice of discipleship as including people with dementia diseases and affirms their calling and gifts.

Chapter 9 identifies dementia diseases as both challenges and opportunities for the church. The church is an alternative community to those in prevailing culture and pushes the margins to include the vulnerable and powerless. Do people with dementia diseases really belong? Does their presence and do their gifts matter to the congregation? What does it mean to "bear one another's burdens and so fulfill the law of Christ"?

Medical and financial realities related to dementia receive considerable attention; however, little attention is paid to the spiritual needs of people with the diseases and their caregivers. Chapter 10 identifies spiritual needs and calls for congregations and pastors to respond to those needs with meaningful relationships and practices.

Chapter 11 puts the spotlight on *death* and *grieving*. Dementia diseases are progressive and fatal; therefore, loss, death, and grieving are integral to the entire process. Dealing with perpetual and ambiguous grieving takes a toll on all involved, and congregations and pastors play critical roles in "the long goodbye." Rituals of grieving have added relevance as does the conviction that "love endures."

The final chapter pulls together themes discussed throughout the book and the implications for *pastoral theology* and *pastoral care* by clergy and congregations. Engaging in theological reflection while accompanying persons on the long and treacherous journey with dementia diseases can lead to profound experiences of divine grace by individuals and communities. Resources and partners are available to accompany us on the journey and equip us for compassionate ministry.

Chapter 1

Dementia through
a Medical Lens

Introduction

The words exploded like a bombshell when spoken by the doctor: "frontotemporal dementia!" Though we knew something was amiss in Linda's thinking, the word *dementia* had been avoided. The term conjured up too many fears, negative stereotypes, and foreboding possibilities to be used to identify the reason for Linda's symptoms.

Many people I talk with confess they fear Alzheimer's and other forms of dementia more than cancer or any other disease; and this fear increases with age and as they come to know people in their circles who are diagnosed. Denial, therefore, is an understandable response.

Furthermore, the stigma attached to dementia contributes to denial. "I'd rather lose my life than my mind" is a familiar expression. In a society that places priority on intellectual acumen and communication skills, cognitive and language degeneration are often viewed as worse than death itself. Frequently heard remarks by people in early-stage dementia include "I'm stupid," "I'm crazy," "I hate myself."

The fear of lost relationships and isolation contributes to dread of the word *dementia*. Symptoms frequently include loss of social skills as behavioral filters weaken, making social interaction more difficult. The world becomes smaller as the circle of relationships diminishes. Potential loneliness and isolation loom ahead.

Much of the explosiveness of the word *dementia* originates in misunderstanding or lack of basic knowledge of the diseases that fall under the term. Separated from medical information, the term can be demeaning. It is sometimes used to insult, discount, or negatively judge another. "She's demented, so don't pay attention to anything she says." Or referring to a person who commits a serious crime as "demented" promotes the notion that people with cognitive diseases are dangerous. People with dementia are not criminals or "stupid" or without gifts and talents. They are individual persons with diseases of the brain.

A medical lens is an important means of countering such misunderstanding and perhaps lessening the denial and stigma associated with dementia.

Definitions: *Dementia* as an Umbrella Term

What is *dementia*? The term as widely used implies that dementia is a disease when, in fact, it is an umbrella term covering a constellation of symptoms of underlying diseases. The precise medical definition from the World Health Organization's International Classification of Diseases and Related Health Problems, tenth edition (ICD-10), is as follows:

> Dementia is a syndrome due to disease of the brain, usually of a chronic or progressive nature, in which there is disturbance of multiple higher cortical functions, including memory, thinking, orientation, comprehension, calculation, learning capacity, language, and judgement. Consciousness is not clouded. The impairments of cognitive function are commonly accompanied, and occasionally preceded, by deterioration in emotional control, social behavior, or motivation. This syndrome occurs in Alzheimer's disease, in cerebrovascular disease, and in other conditions primarily or secondarily affecting the brain.[1]

The National Institutes of Health defines *dementia* based on the cognitive losses, as follows:

> Dementia is the loss of cognitive functioning—thinking, remembering, and reasoning—and behavioral abilities to such an extent that it interferes with a person's daily life and activities. These functions include memory,

language skills, visual perception, problem solving, self-management, and the ability to focus and pay attention.[2]

These definitions for dementia include several important components. First, dementia is a *syndrome,* or group of related symptoms, that characterize a particular abnormality or condition of the brain. Therefore, dementia refers to symptoms or manifestations of underlying physiological conditions. Several diseases manifest themselves in the symptoms that fall under the umbrella of dementia.

Second, the symptoms that manifest themselves in dementia correlate with pathologies in the brain. They are diseases of the brain, as heart disease is a disease of the heart. There should be no more stigma assigned to people with diseases of the brain than to those with diseases of the heart or liver or kidneys. They are all impairments of bodily organs.

There is a difference in how dementia impacts a person, compared with other embodied diseases, however. Diseases of the brain adversely affect the person's thinking, perception, behavior, and control. In the early and middle stages of her disease, Linda was embarrassed that she couldn't remember people's names or keep up with conversations and that she would often say inappropriate things. She felt "stupid" and ashamed. Others may have considered her uninterested or even rude. But such behaviors were beyond my wife's control. Those negative behaviors were the disease, not Linda!

Separating the symptoms of disease from the identity of the person is crucial if the stigma is to be removed and for persons with dementia to be socially accepted. Much of the stigma attached to dementia results from the assumption that the negative symptoms reflect a lack of attentiveness, control, or volition on the part of the person with the condition. Medical information says otherwise.

Also, dementia is not to be confused with the normal cognitive decline that may accompany aging. The aging process affects the total physical organism, including the brain. So-called senior moments—temporary forgetfulness and lapses in recollection—are universal and normal. We all forget at times where we left our car keys; but a person with a brain disease may very well forget what a key or a car is. Furthermore, we can compensate for aging's memory lapses, whereas a person with Alzheimer's or other forms of dementia will be unable to make such adjustments.

More precise language with fewer negative connotations is needed. Some emerging possibilities in medical literature include "neurocognitive disorders," "cognitive impairment," "degenerative brain disease," or simply "brain diseases." Whatever term is used, it is important to emphasize that the symptoms manifested originate in the malfunction or degeneration of the brain and are not to be equated with behavioral choices or a person's character.

The Brain: Remarkable and Mysterious

Although it weighs only about three pounds, the human brain holds incalculable information and vast power, affecting every aspect of the human body. Our brains significantly initiate, regulate, and monitor our thoughts and actions. The brain's capacity to store and process information and experiences far exceeds its physical size. It, therefore, is understandable that the renowned Dutch neuroscientist D. H. Swaab would declare: "Everything we think, do, and refrain from doing is determined by the brain. The constructions of this fantastic machine determine our potential, our limitations, and our characters; *we are our brains*."[3]

Swaab's perspective as to the centrality of the brain in human identity mirrors the long-accepted hypothesis expressed by Hippocrates (c. 460–c. 370 BCE), considered the father of medicine:

> It should be widely known that the brain, and the brain alone, is the source of our pleasures, joys, laughter, and amusement, as well as our sorrow, pain, grief, and tears. It is especially the organ we use to think and learn, see and hear, to distinguish the bad from the good, and the pleasant from the unpleasant. The brain is also the seat of madness and delirium, of the fears and terrors which assail us.[4]

Theology challenges the mechanistic view of the mind and human identity; nevertheless, the relationship between the brain and our feelings and actions is indisputable. The more we learn about the brain, the more questions emerge, and mystery deepens.

The brain consists of approximately one hundred billion neurons, even more glial cells, one hundred trillion synapses, and a hundred billion capillaries. It is an enormously complex organ, and scientists are only beginning to fathom its composition, functioning, and influence.

Medical imaging technology has significantly increased the ability to study the brain and the complex interactions taking place within. Nevertheless, the brain remains a profound mystery. Jeff W. Lichtman, MD and PhD, Professor of Molecular and Cellular Biology at Harvard, reflects in a *National Geographic* segment that we have only begun to understand the brain. He often asks students, "If understanding everything we need to know about the brain equals one mile, how far do you think we have walked?" The usual answers are "three quarters," "one half," or "one quarter." The eminent researcher responds, "I think about three inches."[5]

Dementia can be described as "brain failure" or "degeneration of the brain" or "malfunction of the brain." The failure, degeneration, or malfunction results from diseases that affect the neurons, synapses, cells, and capillaries in the brain.

The one hundred billion neurons in the brain live to communicate with one another. Each neuron connects to thousands of other neurons through chemical messengers called neurotransmitters. During any one moment, millions of signals are passed from neuron to neuron and are speeding through pathways in the brain.

In order to stay healthy, neurons need to communicate with one another, receive adequate nutrition (oxygen and glucose) through blood supply, and be able to repair themselves. The disorders that cause dementia disrupt these functions of the neurons. While each disorder has a different mechanism or cause, dementia results because

- *connections* between neurons are interrupted or lost;
- neurons cannot metabolize nutrients and/or blood supply is interrupted;
- neurons cannot repair themselves; and
- neurons die.

– 5 –

The specific symptoms of the underlying diseases tend to reflect the areas of the brain being damaged. For example, damage in the hippocampus results in trouble forming and retaining memories. Damage to the frontal lobes results in difficulty with "executive functions" such as organizing, sequencing, and making decisions. Since much of the brain's composition and functioning remains a mystery, scientists are only beginning to identify the various malfunctions underlying the symptoms.

Types of Dementia

When the doctor shared with us Linda's diagnosis, we only heard the one word, *dementia*. We had never heard the term *frontotemporal dementia*. We recognized Alzheimer's as a dreaded form of dementia, and we knew of elderly persons whose memory loss and confusion were attributed to "hardening of the arteries" or atherosclerosis. The moisture in the doctor's eyes should have alerted us that *frontotemporal* added gravity to *dementia*. We were soon to learn that many diseases fall under the *dementia* umbrella.

Currently, there is no single test to diagnose any of the diseases that cause dementia. Rather, they are diagnosed primarily through the person's symptoms and by ruling out other causes. Sometimes a person can have symptoms that appear to be dementia but are caused by other conditions. Medication, infections, nutritional deficiencies, an injury such as a concussion, depression, or severe emotional trauma can each result in acute or chronic confusion, memory impairment, and language difficulties. These treatable conditions must first be ruled out before a diagnosis of Alzheimer's or a related disease is made.

A thorough evaluation involves recording a detailed medical history, conducting physical and neurological exams, and administering psychological and cognitive tests. Laboratory tests can help find treatable causes such as thyroid problems or vitamin deficiencies. Brain scans such as magnetic resonance imagining (MRI) can reveal tumors, strokes and other vascular changes, and shrinkage within the brain.[6]

Advancement is being made in identifying biomarkers that signal the disease, but these are now used primarily in research settings. They include advanced brain imaging techniques such as positron emission tomography (PET) scans to identify glucose metabolism in the brain and cerebrospinal fluid (CSF) evaluation to identify proteins that are characteristic of Alzheimer's disease. Genetic testing may be ordered if there is a strong family history of disease or if a rare form of dementia is suspected.[7]

Treatments and Medical Challenges

No cure or effective treatments currently exist for Alzheimer's and other dementias. Medications commonly prescribed for Alzheimer's disease, such as Aricept (donepezil) and Namenda (memantine), may decrease symptoms and enhance functioning for a time in some people. Other medications are used to control behavioral and mood symptoms such as agitation, anxiety, aggression, and depression.[8]

While research increasingly reveals the complexities of the genetic, environmental, and lifestyle factors that contribute to degenerative brain diseases, the underlying causes are not yet fully understood. Known risk factors for developing Alzheimer's and related diseases include: advancing age, vascular disease, diabetes, Down syndrome, head injury, and genetics.[9] How these and other factors under investigation influence disease progression and interact with each other are questions yet to be answered by the researchers.

The most promising current efforts are directed toward prevention and delaying the onset of the diseases. Protective factors are summed up in what the physician advised us, "What's good for the heart is good for the brain." Maintaining good cardiovascular health through exercise and a healthful diet, engaging in lifelong learning, and staying active and involved with others appear to play a role in maintaining brain health.[10] It is important to note that genetics and other factors can result in brain disease despite our best efforts at prevention.

Characteristics and Consequences

All sensations, movements, thoughts, and feelings result from signals transmitted through billions of neurons in the brain.[11] Our perception of and interaction with the world depends upon the functioning of the brain. Therefore, every aspect of our existence is potentially impacted when disease invades the brain—self-image, memory, capacities, and relationships.

As stated previously, the specific consequences of the pathology depend on the portion of the brain affected. The diseases are progressive, and the severity of the symptoms increases as cells die. The diseases are fatal with the life expectancy after diagnosis as brief as two years and as long as twenty years.[12] Death often occurs as the indirect consequence of the underlying pathology, such as a fall, pneumonia or other infection, or inability to swallow.

While there are common manifestations of brain pathologies, each person with dementia is unique. A common adage is "if you've met one person with dementia, you've met one person with dementia." Multiple factors affect the symptoms and manifestations, and each person must be dealt with as an individual. Furthermore, the symptoms vary in their duration and persistence. Even persons in the severe stage of Alzheimer's or another form of dementia may mysteriously have short lucid moments. "[Kissing] the joy as it flies by"[13] is the challenge of caregivers and family members as they journey with the person with dementia.

The consequences of dementia far exceed those experienced by the person diagnosed. Alzheimer's and other forms of dementia significantly impact families, communities, and the broader society. In fact, the Alzheimer's Association reports that "more than 16 million Americans provide unpaid care for people with Alzheimer's or other dementias." The vast majority of these are family members. Many of these caregivers are so-called sandwich generation caregivers who are responsible not only for an aging parent's care but also for children.

According to that same 2019 report from the Alzheimer's Association, the healthcare and long-term care costs for individuals with Alzheimer's and other forms of dementia are estimated at $290 billion.[14] The total out-of-pocket expenses for these family caregivers is expected to exceed $63 billion, or 22 percent of their medical payments.[15] The lifetime cost of caring for an individual with dementia is estimated at $357.650.[16] With the significant increase in the number of people with Alzheimer's and other forms of dementia, the monetary costs will dramatically escalate.

The most traumatic consequences, however, are less quantifiable. They have to do with the changes and demands placed on family members and caregivers. In addition to the added stress of financially caring for a family member, the physical and emotional demands are enormous. Evidence exists linking dementia-caregiving to increased levels of depression and anxiety, social isolation, and potential physical health decline.[17]

The consequences of dementia for both patients and caregivers are influenced by more than the pathology of the brain. Additional factors include the support systems in place, degree of stigma attached to Alzheimer's and other forms of dementia, and how personhood is defined. If we are our brains, then degeneration of the brain means diminished personhood, loss of self.

Reducing people to their brains is an unwarranted medical conclusion rooted largely in the outdated Cartesian mind/body dichotomy and notion of individual autonomy. Emerging neuroscience, the social sciences, and theology push against the notion that we are our brains and that memory is far more complex than the functioning of brain cells.

Conclusion

"I hate myself" was Linda's often-repeated expression following that fateful November afternoon in 2009 when we heard the doctor pronounce the diagnosis of frontotemporal dementia. Frequently thereafter, as she struggled to think and speak clearly, she called herself "stupid," "crazy," "no good," "worthless." Her self-image and confidence as well as her recollections waned. Her self-concept, relationships, social networks, abilities, and capacities diminished: all the result of what was taking place in the small organ called the *brain*.

The negative consequences have been far-reaching. Yet, there have been positive consequences as well resulting from several factors. First, accepting that her dementia is caused by a disease increases my perspective and patience. Gradually, when she was confused and unable to express her thoughts, she would say, "My brain isn't working right." That was progress!

It wasn't that she was inattentive or unconcerned; her brain wasn't working properly! As I persistently reminded her, "You have a disease of the brain; I have a disease of the heart! But together we make a whole."

We also learned that even the mind and memory are more than the mechanisms operating in the brain. Memory is more than the recollection of data. The mind includes more than recall of events, information, and experiences. As we shall see in the next chapter, memory is complex and multifaceted with numerous physiological, biological, relational, and theological components.

Chapter 2

Dementia: Mind, Memory, and God

Introduction

"I'm losing my mind," Linda repeatedly said as her memory faded and she had difficulty making decisions. The words were spoken in frustration, fear, and embarrassment. I had the uneasy feeling that she felt she was losing more than the ability to recall information or to make a choice on a restaurant menu. She was afraid of losing herself!

I sensed the loss of my life partner as changes in the brain inexorably chipped away familiar traits and ordinary abilities. I recall telling a friend during the early stages, "Linda's losing her mind; and I'm losing her, a brain cell at a time." Her mind and her identity were inextricably bound together.

We have bought into the long-standing perception that we are our minds, and our minds are confined to the brain. The notion is pervasive and widespread, and it accounts for much of the stigma and marginalization associated with dementia. Here are some comments I've heard:

"He's out of his mind and there's no use visiting him," said a pastor.

"I know you must miss Linda since she lost her mind," commented a neighbor.

"If I lose my mind, I might as well be dead," remarked an acquaintance.

"I won't be worth anything if I lose my mind," announced a professor.

"Without our memory and our mind, we are nothing," exclaimed a medical student.

"I'm afraid of losing my mind. You lose your identity, your sense of who you are, where you are," stated author Stephen King in an interview.

"I do not want to lose my mind. I hope to die from my own hand before this, with my mind in tact," reads a note from a neighbor with Alzheimer's.

Little wonder we fear dementia! Such comments reflect a culture of stigma, fear, isolation, and neglect. The roots of the word *dementia* come from the Latin words *de,* or "without," and *mens,* or "mind," which come together to mean "without mind." Dementia and madness have gotten intertwined in public perception, and to be referred to as "demented" is an insult. Merriam-Webster lists the following among the synonyms for *demented: batty, bonkers, crackbrained, cracked, crackpot, cranky, crazed, crazy, cuckoo, daffy, deranged, insane, kooky, loco, looney, lunatic, mad, nuts, psycho, screwy, unbalanced, unhinged, wacko!*

The language associated with cognitive degeneration reflects the challenge faced by persons with diseases that fall under the umbrella of "dementia." The language also exposes our limited comprehension of what we mean by *mind* and *memory.*

Do people with cognitive impairment actually lose their "minds" and their "memories"? What is the relationship among our brains, our minds, our memories, and our identity and worth? How might theology broaden and deepen our understanding of *mind* and *memory*? These are among the questions we turn to in this chapter.

What Is the Mind?

The question has occupied attention of philosophers for at least two millennia: What is the mind? How does one account for such capacities as remembering the past, comprehending the world around us, integrating the past with the present and the future, making decisions and evaluating the consequences of those decisions?

Greek philosopher Plato (c. 427–c. 327 BCE) recognized the complexity of what constitutes the mind, its nature, and its function. He acknowledged the mind's mystery in such questions as these: "Do we learn with one part of us, feel angry with another, and desire the pleasures of eating and sex with another? Or do we employ our mind as a whole when our energies are employed in any of these ways?"[1]

The complexity and even confusion as to the nature of the human mind is evident in the way the term *mind* is defined in contemporary dictionaries. Merriam-Webster's medical definition is as follows: "the element or complex of elements in an individual that feels, perceives, thinks, wills, and especially reasons; the conscious mental events and capabilities in an organism; the organized conscious and unconscious adaptive mental activity of an organism."[2] The synonyms for *mind* include *brain, intelligence, intellect, thoughts,* and *attention.*

Central to the discussion is the relationship between the brain and the mind. Are they one and the same? Any discussion of the mind raises the specter of the mind/body dualism with its accompanying mechanistic understanding of the body.[3] It is an ancient dualism present in many cultures—the separation of the material from the spiritual, the soul from the body.

The materialist perspective limits the mind to biological functioning within the organ called the brain. Although our understanding of the brain is limited, as we saw in the last chapter, some assume that once our knowledge of the brain is complete, we will have grasped the secrets of the mind. The current mystery lies simply in our lack of understanding; and studies of the substance of the physical brain will unveil the mystery of the mind.

Philosophers of the mind, however, postulate that the mind extends beyond the confines of the human brain of individuals. René Descartes held that the mind is a nonphysical substance and involves consciousness and self-awareness, while the brain is the location of intelligence.[4]

Contemporary neurologists, philosophers, and theologians acknowledge the difficulty in defining the *mind.* John Swinton, a pastoral theologian with experience as a psychiatric nurse, states the problem:

> Why would we assume that the person's mind has gone (or that his thinking is irreparably impaired) when we are in fact deeply unclear about what *any-*

one's mind is and the state of *anyone's* thinking. . . . To suggest that a person with dementia has "lost his mind" may actually relate to the inadequacies of the particular stories that we're using to make sense of our encounters with those who bear the name "dementia."[5]

movie)

Living with someone with dementia provides ongoing experience that confirms the impossibility of determining what is going on in another's mind. Amid confusion and incoherence often come unexpected and inexplicable moments of clarity and articulation. So, to say that another has "lost her mind" is presumptuous and speculative and exposes our faulty understanding as much as the impairment of the other.

Mind in Christian Theology

Mind plays a role in Christian theology. When asked about the greatest commandment, Jesus responded, "You shall love the Lord your God with all your heart, and with all your soul, and with all your mind" (Matt 22:37). Commentators and preachers frequently point out the addition of the word *mind* to the ancient Shema from which Jesus quoted, indicating that we are to love God with our intellect.

In the English translations of Apostle Paul's letters, the word *mind* is used in these two prominent passages:

Do not be conformed to this world, but be transformed by the renewing of your minds, so that you may discern what is the will of God—what is good and acceptable and perfect. (Rom 12:2)

Let the same mind be in you that was in Christ Jesus. (Phil 2:5)

The use of the term translated *mind* in the New Testament pushes us beyond the contemporary notion that our mind is limited to the intellectual, cognitive activity of an individual's brain. The Greek word for mind is *nous* and its variants. While it includes thinking, the meaning is much broader and more comprehensive than cognition; and the idea that humans are a collection of body parts, with what we consider intellect being contained in one part, is alien to both Hebrew Scriptures and the New Testament.

For one thing, the Bible emerges from the community, is written to the community, and is to be lived within community. Therefore, passages that refer to the mind must be read in context of communal thinking rather than individual autonomy.

Modern concepts of individualism and personal autonomy are foreign to the worlds of the Bible. As New Testament scholar Susan Eastman documents, none of Paul's anthropological terms can be understood in an individualistic, autonomous, isolated way; they require community.[6] "To lose my mind" in the context of the Bible and Pauline theology would be to lose community and to be defined apart from the intricate and integral relationships of which I am an inseparable part.

It is precisely the understanding of person as an autonomous, self-sufficient, self-contained individual that contributes to the devastation of Alzheimer's and other forms of dementia. Individualism, then, undergirds the practices of isolation and dehumanization of people with dementia and contributes to their diminished self-worth expressed in the fear of "losing my mind."

In contrast to individualism, Christian theology declares that the mind originates and is held in community in a web of interdependent relationships. Transformation by "the renewing of your minds" is a *communal* call, meaning it is fulfilled within community. "Renewing of mind" does include a renewal or transformation of thinking or way of intellectually understanding, but it is more.

Paul's use of the term in Philippians 2:1-5 pushes toward a much broader definition and understanding. He uses the Greek word *phronēsi,* which has a more holistic sense. As Stephen Fowl suggests, *phronesis* (mind) refers to one's way of being in the world, orientation toward life and reality.[7] Having "the mind that was in Christ Jesus" involves character—humility, servanthood, obedience to God, "self-emptying." The reward of such a mind lies not in the capacities of the individual but from being "bestowed" value, a "name that is above every name" (Phil 2:9).

Paul's honoring of "the lesser parts of the body" further supports a holistic and interrelational concept of the mind. The metaphor of "the body" in 1 Corinthians 12–14 challenges the notion of individualism, personal autonomy, and elevation of intellect as superior to all gifts or qualities. Indeed, the smallest and most insignificant are indispensable members of the whole. An injured or impaired brain is no less a valued part of the whole!

To summarize, defining cognitive degeneration or impairment as tantamount to "losing the mind" is presumptuous, misleading, and demeaning. We don't know precisely what the mind is, but we do know that it is more than the information, knowledge, and functions stored in the brain. Theologically, we affirm that the mind cannot be severed from the relational and interrelatedness of human community, and it represents a total orientation toward and involvement in the world. Additionally, the importance or value of the mind is unrelated to the intellectual acumen of the individual but has more to do with qualities of character, particularly humility being bestowed with honor by God and held within community.

Memory and the Brain

All forms of dementia have this symptom in common: the impairment of memory. Forgetting is one of the earliest and most frustrating signs of Alzheimer's and other forms of dementia. In a sense, we are our memories, and the inability to recall experiences, information, and relationships threatens our sense of self and our relationship with the world.

Memory, however, is more complex than is commonly assumed. *Memory* is defined as follows in a widely used medical dictionary:

1. the mental faculty or power that enables one to retain and to recall, through unconscious associative processes, previously experienced sensations, impressions, ideas, concepts, and all information that has been consciously learned.

2. the reservoir of all past experiences and knowledge that may be recollected or recalled at will.

3. the recollection of a past event, idea, sensation, or previously learned knowledge.[8]

The technical definition acknowledges the mystery of how memory works. The brain is sometimes compared to a computer hard drive in which information is stored and recalled with the click of a mouse. In such an analogy, diseases that contribute to dementia are "viruses" that slow down the collecting and processing of data, or destroy it altogether. The definition above, however, indicates that the faculty for retaining data depends upon "unconscious associative processes." In other words, there is more to memory than can be captured by mechanistic comparison to a computer.

Memory certainly has to do with "the ways in which the brain captures, records, processes, and retains information that it gathers through experience."[9] As Swinton points out, St. Augustine understood memory to be essentially a "storehouse for countless images," located in the private space within an individual. That storehouse of memories is synonymous with the mind and constitutes the self.[10]

If memory is simply a storehouse or archive of experiences and data residing within the mind of an individual, then one may conclude that the loss of memory is the loss of self. Indeed, many in our society conclude that we are our memories, and diminished memories means diminished self. David Keck, who cared for his mother with Alzheimer's, writes:

> It is impossible to distinguish between ourselves and our memories.... *We are our memories,* and without them we have but a physical resemblance to that person we each suppose ourselves to be.... The apparent dissolution of the mnemonic capacities...raises most serious and profound questions about human existence.[11]

A closer look at how memory works, however, challenges the idea that "we are our memories" and that the loss of memories means the loss of self. Scientists are documenting the complexity involved in recording, retaining, recalling, and integrating experiences, images, and information within the brain. They have only scratched the surface in understanding how the neurons (brain cells), synapses (connections), and the structure of the brain interact to create, retain, recall, and shape memories.

A growing number of neuroscientists and psychologists suggest that physical metaphors for memory, such as computer, filing cabinet, photographic plates, storehouse, and so on, are misleading. Charles Fernyhough, professor of psychology at Durham University in the United Kingdom, writes:

> Memories are not physical things or possessions that one has or doesn't have. They are mental constructions, created in the present moment, according to the demands of the present....Memory is more like a *habit*, a process of constructing something from its parts, in similar but subtly changing ways each time, whenever the occasion arises.[12]

Memory functions more like an artist than a technician, a poet more than a stenographer. Memories are combinations of recalled events and imaginative interpretations of those events. Each recollection is influenced by the context in which the remembered event, or relationship, or experience takes place. Memories, therefore, are dynamic and fluid rather than static and fixed.

As an artist or poet may be inspired by a present sensory experience, memory may be stimulated by a smell, sight, sound, or touch. The rekindled memory is now filtered through the current context, which reconstitutes the recall and expression of the past event or experience. Memory, then, is always being reconstructed.

The creation and reconstruction of memories involves the whole body, not simply the hippocampus. The body remembers—cells, atoms, organs, muscles! How another person is appropriating memories within their current reality is impossible for us to totally comprehend. Even our own memories are being appropriated and reconstructed through unconscious interactions within our own bodies and in relationship with the world around us.

People with dementia have memory! The ability to recall, retain, access, integrate, and express specific memories is affected by the health of the brain. However, those who live with people with dementia can provide multiple examples of unexpected recognition and recollection. Attentiveness to the persons with dementia and knowledge of their stories enable us to connect with and appropriate their memories.

Even though Linda is in the severe stage of her disease and is unable to recall our experiences together over more than a half century, she regularly exhibits signs of "remembering." Occasionally a certain twinkle in her eyes seems to indicate that she remembers me as her husband. Other times she calls me "daddy," especially when I am feeding her. Apparently, the recollection of being cared for is reconstructed and I become her father.

People in the memory care facility form community and construct the present from their habits from the past. One man who is twenty years older than Linda "remembered" her as his "sister," and he looked after her as he had likely cared for a younger sibling. Another resident was a retired nurse who made her rounds each evening and insisted on taking care of residents who were more infirm. Often behaviors that staff or family members consider destructive or difficult represent residents acting out of memories that are being reconstructed in their present context. They are living in their current context with memories or habits formed in previous contexts.

Memory as Communal

Thus far we have discussed memory as a faculty held within the individual. Just as *mind* cannot be defined as existing within an autonomous, self-contained individual, neither can memory! Memories originate in, are retained within, and are nurtured by relationships. We all are shaped by the collective memories of families, cultures, nations, and local communities. Our individual recollections are influenced by the memories of the communities of which we are part.

Today, as I write, marks the seventeenth anniversary of terrorist attacks in 2001. While each person may recall where he or she was when the attacks occurred and the individual feelings and interpretations of the events, the entire nation pauses to remember. Monuments have been built and liturgies developed to honor those who died in the attacks but also as means of preserving memories. While some individuals may have forgotten the events of September 11, the memory is held by and appropriated by the total community.

Most people remember only a small fraction of the details of their past and depend upon others to fill in the gaps of their own recollection. When my mother died at age ninety-six, memories of my early childhood were lost. She held the memories of my first few years. We all hold memories for one another. Our family members, friends, associates, neighbors, teachers, even casual acquaintances have impressions and memories of us that are outside our own recollection.

Persons with dementia, therefore, only lose their memories if they are isolated from community. Although Linda cannot recall past experiences and may have forgotten her family and friends, we remember her, and we are now the stewards of her memories. There are some memories held only by the individual and those may be erased by diseases of the brain. From a theological perspective, only God remembers the whole of one's life.

Toward a Theology of Memory[13]

Remember is a familiar admonition in Jewish and Christian Scriptures. At the heart of the faith, according to the Hebrew Scriptures, is remembering the mighty acts of God, especially in the deliverance from Egyptian slavery. The people are cautioned, "take care that you do not forget the LORD, who brought you out of the land of Egypt, out of the house of slavery" (Deut 6:12). The psalmist declares, "Remember the wonderful works he has done" (Ps 105:5).

At the center of the Christian faith is the act of remembrance in the sacrament of Holy Communion. "Do this in remembrance of me," Jesus directed the disciples. Both the exodus as reenacted in the Passover and God's mighty acts in Jesus Christ represented in the Lord's Supper are means of remembering. What about those who cannot recall these pivotal stories?

Three points must be made. First, the admonition to remember is directed toward the community. It is the community that is to keep the memory alive of God's acts of salvation in the deliverance from slavery and in the life, teaching, death, and resurrection of Jesus. It takes the entire community to remember! If one member forgets, the community remembers for him or her. As we shall see later, the church is the community of remembrance and the stewards of memories.

Second, the admonition to remember is more than a summons to recall an event; it is an invitation to participate in the lived reality. Remembering the deliverance from Egyptian slavery is to share liberation in the present; and as we partake of the bread and drink the wine "in remembrance," we share in Christ's life, death, and resurrection as the community of Christ.

Third, the central focus of Scripture is God's memory, not human recollection. God's being and action in relationship with creation, especially humanity, is the central theme of the biblical story and Christian tradition. Human beings, made in the image of God, have been incorporated into God's story. Therein lies our origin, identity, purpose, and destiny.

The bedrock theological affirmation is this: We are created by God, known by God, redeemed by God, remembered by God! We know only a fraction of ourselves; God knows us totally, completely (cf. Ps 139). "For now we see in a mirror, dimly, but then we will see face to face. Now I know only in part; then I will know fully, even as I have been fully known" (1 Cor 13:12).

Such an affirmation has significant implications when considering people with dementia. For one thing, it challenges the notion that persons with dementia lose their identity if they lose their memory. Our identity lies in God's memory, not our personal memory. Additionally, our identity is in process and is fully known only by God! Who am I? Only God knows!

How are we to understand God's memory? To speak of "God's memory" requires that we think outside neurology and physiology. After all, God has no physical organ called the brain. John Swinton summarizes what it means for God to remember in these words: "God's memory has to do with *sustenance* and *action*. To be remembered is to be sustained; to be forgotten is to cease to exist. To be remembered is to be the recipient of divine action."[14]

The Bible contains multiple references to God "remembering." Here is a sampling of those references.

> When I bring clouds over the earth and the bow is seen in the clouds, I will remember my covenant that is between me and you and every living creature of all flesh; and the waters shall never again become a flood to destroy all flesh. (Gen 9:14-15)

God heard their groaning, and God remembered his covenant with Abraham, Isaac, and Jacob. God looked upon the Israelites, and God took notice of them. (Exod 2:24-25)

Can a woman forget her nursing child,
> or show no compassion for the child of her womb?
Even these may forget,
> yet I will not forget you.
See, I have inscribed you on the palms of my hands. (Isa 49:15-16) *tats*

Nevertheless he regarded their distress
> when he heard their cry.
For their sake he remembered his covenant,
> and showed compassion according to the abundance
> of his steadfast love. (Ps 106:44-45)

Two prominent components of God's remembering are *covenant* and *action*. God remembers God's covenant, God's promises. But such remembrance is more than recollection or reminder; it is action on behalf of the fulfillment of covenant. God's memory and God's action are inextricably bound together. To be remembered by God is to be known, sustained, and loved by God.

God's memory is the inexhaustible source, the infinite fountain from which flows all existence. It is within God's memory that "we live and move and have our being" (Acts 17:28). John Swinton declares, "Human memory is nothing more (and nothing less) than one mode of participation in the memory of God, which is our true memory and our only real source of identity and hope."[15]

We have been incorporated into God's memory and unfolding action in creation, liberation, restoration, reconciliation, and transformation. Therein lies our identity and our destiny.

Conclusion

Living with Linda during the severe stage of her dementia is filled with surprises. Presumably her memories are being inexorably erased and her mind is being lost in the dark abyss of dying neurons, disconnected synapses, and shrinking brain matter. Much of the time she seems to be in another world into which we cannot enter and from which she cannot escape. It's a world of incoherent sounds and sleeping silence, a world of unpredictable outbursts and inexplicable behavior.

I often stand or sit beside her bed and watch her sleep or twist her head back and forth as her scrambled words flow forth. I wonder: Where is she? Who is she now? What is in her mind? Does she remember me at all? Have all the memories of our almost sixty years together and her eight decades been erased?

Then, without warning comes a fleeting moment of clarity, connection, recognition. As an ineffable mystery, there appears a familiar smile or twinkle in the eye or even a spoken, "There you are!" or "Hello!" Or it may be in the squeeze of the hand as I pull away, as though she is holding onto someone she knows. She's still here, I think to myself.

Even when there are no visible signs of recognition or recall and it appears that she is lost in a world of emptiness, I remember who she is to me and to our family and to her countless friends. We hold her memories! She is integral to our identity, our memories, our minds.

But even more mysterious and wondrous, she is an integral part of a transcendent story. The God who knew her when she "was being made in secret, intricately woven in the depths of the earth" and whose "eyes beheld [her] unformed substance" (Ps 139:15-16) holds her in the divine memory.

— *fetus*

Chapter 3

Dementia as Theological Challenge and Opportunity

Lens

Introduction

During a Maundy Thursday service several years ago, I noticed a poignant change in Linda. As we moved forward to receive Communion by intinction, she was obviously confused. She didn't know what to do. She had received the bread and wine countless times, but now it was strange to her. I took the bread, dipped it into the chalice, and placed it in her mouth. The look on her face was one of mournful bewilderment.

As we returned home, she began to cry. "I don't understand!" she said. I tried to explain that we had been to Communion and remembered Jesus's Last Supper and the Sacrament. Shockingly, she asked, "Who's Jesus?"

Linda was trained as a Christian educator, and the church has been central to her life since birth. The beliefs and practices of the Christian community have shaped her and are integral to her worldview, self-perception, identity, and relationships. But dementia slowly chipped away her religious perceptions and practices.

The challenges of dementia are multiple and pervasive. When the brain loses its ability to perceive, process, and communicate, all aspects of living change. Simple tasks become complicated. Words lose their meaning. Memories fade. Thoughts get jumbled. Boundaries crumble. Relationships change. Abstractions become meaningless. Stories disappear.

"What if I forget God?" a retired pastor with early-stage Alzheimer's asked. "What if I lose my beliefs?" Those are only two of the theological questions raised by many people of faith when diseases invade the brain. The question of theodicy and "why?" emerges as families struggle to find meaning and purpose amid persistent losses and disruptions. Longtime religious rituals may lose their meaning or become impossible to practice.

The medical, financial, relational, and family challenges of dementia dominate the literature. Less attention is given to the theological and spiritual challenges and opportunities. Religion consists of creeds, doctrinal affirmations, beliefs, and individual and corporate practices. Brain diseases strip away the ability to comprehend abstract doctrines and creeds. They interfere with liturgical practices and limit social interaction.

David Keck, in his book *Forgetting Whose We Are: Alzheimer's Disease and the Love of God*, contends that dementia is "a theological disease."[1] Keck's point is correct that Alzheimer's disease pushes beyond the medical lens as it impacts the meaning of personhood, wholeness, salvation, sin, and love.

In this chapter, we will consider the theological challenges and opportunities inherent in the struggle with Alzheimer's and other forms of dementia. While diseases of the brain challenge many of the components of religious faith and practice, theology contributes to broader perceptions and provides redemptive resources for living with the diseases.

Limitations of the Medical Lens

During one of Linda's several medical evaluations, a nurse practitioner interpreted the findings. Looking at me, she reviewed the results, indicating that Linda was in mid-stage of her disease. Then she added, still gazing at me, "Mr. Carder, you must understand that your wife is not the person she used to be. The disease is taking her away. She is a shell of the person you have known." As the nurse practitioner continued to describe the disease without ever acknowledging Linda's presence, Linda became increasingly restless. A familiar expressiveness appeared in her eyes. I knew the practitioner was about to learn something she probably missed in medical training.

[Handwritten margin notes:]
1. vindication of divine goodness and providence in view of the existence of evil.
2. the belief in and worship of a superhuman controlling power

Linda straightened up in her chair and stared intently and directly at her. In a harsh voice filled with irritation, she demanded, "Talk to ME!" I smiled and said to the nurse practitioner, "Meet Linda! She is still here!" I commented that Linda is more than the symptoms of her disease and should be treated as a person rather than a constellation of symptoms. I added, "You know her only by her symptoms; I know her by her story. I know the story behind that look and demand."

The limitations of the medical lens are frequently evident in the institutional setting. During a care-planning meeting attended by a physician and others caring for Linda, one person responded to my concern about the inadequate attentiveness, sensitivity, and compassion exhibited by some staff members as they cared for Linda's needs. She remarked rather coldly, "If I need medical care, I want people with the skills to treat my condition; I'm not concerned about their bedside manner."

These two medically trained people reflected the outdated body/soul dualism. They only saw Linda as a diseased brain. Through such a lens, the body is seen as a machine with the brain serving as the motor and transmission. Or, the brain is viewed as a complex computer storing data and programmed to function in prescribed ways. Such a dualism fails to see the broader dimensions of dementia.

Warren Kinghorn, a psychiatrist and theologian, challenges the "mistake" of defining dementia as a "disease of the brain." He writes:

> "Major neurocognitive disorder" names not brain pathology per se but rather how such pathology shows up in the psychological and social life of the person. The characteristic experiences and behaviors of dementia are closely related to characteristic brain disease, but they are not related only to this. They are also related to how the embodied person with dementia is fed, and exercised, and cared for. They are related to social context and environment, such that people with little social support may appear more "diseased" far earlier than those who are embedded in richer contexts of support and care. They are related to the mundane realities of architecture and built environment. Dementia, like all mental disorders (and, arguably, many general medical disorders), is a biosocial phenomenon, reflecting not only disease of the brain but also the way that these brain processes are received in culture, relationship, and society (Kitwood, 1997). Recognition

of this is important, because excessive focus on dementia as a "brain disease" not only leads to fatalism among those who are diagnosed, but also to the legitimization of socially marginalizing care practices. If people with dementia are suffering from irremediably broken brains, then why not house them in the most efficient "facilities" possible?[2]

If "we are our brains," then diminished brain cells translate into becoming less of a person. The medical lens focuses on individual autonomy while largely ignoring the social dimensions of personhood, thereby contributing to isolation and marginalization. Defining persons by pathological symptoms fosters fear and neglect of those with neurological degeneration. If the person with the disease no longer recognizes us and doesn't remember our presence, why visit or befriend? Many people in memory care units seldom receive visits from family members, pastors, and friends. As a daughter exclaimed: "What's the use to visit? She just isn't the mother I have known. Her brain is gone!"

As we have seen in the previous chapter, memory itself is more than recollections stored in the brain. We are social creatures whose identities are intertwined with family, friends, and a large network of relationships. Theology broadens the lens beyond a mechanistic, body/soul dualism and places human identity and existence within a mysterious and complex web of mutually dependent relationships and interactions.

Theology as Broader Lens

When Linda was first diagnosed, coping with the medical reality occupied our attention. Admittedly, the future looked bleak as we were warned by medical personnel and literature of impending losses and cognitive degeneration. Planning for the future, moving near our daughters, and grappling with advancing symptoms left little energy for theological reflection on what was happening to us.

Yet, questions unanswered by medical science emerged. Where is God? What does it mean to be human when the capacity to remember and think disintegrates? What is the *imago Dei*? What does salvation mean in this context? Can Linda be a disciple of Jesus if she forgets who Jesus is? Is there anything that endures? What does hope mean for us? How will we relate to the church? What resources of our faith can sustain us amid all the changes and losses?

As I was a pastor, bishop, and seminary professor, theological reflection has been central to my life and vocation. These fundamental theological questions have occupied my study and reflection for more than five decades:

- Who is God? Belief in the existence of God is insufficient; the nature or character of God is fundamental.

- Where is God? What are the manifestations of God's presence?

- What is God doing? What is the mission of God—the *missio Dei*?

- What is the appropriate response to the nature, presence, and mission of God?

Such questions represent another lens through which to view reality. They cannot be answered with empirical and measurable data. They presume a transcendent dimension within which the empirical and measurable exist. Theology refers to the critical reflection on the nature, presence, and mission or activity of this Transcendent One and the meaning of religious ideas and practices.

Karl Barth suggests that Scripture is the doorway into a strange new world.[3] Barth reminds us that the stories of the Bible provide a new lens through which to view reality. In the Bible's stories, we locate our own stories. As we enter the world of Hebrew slaves on their journey to the promised land and exiles in their captivity, we locate our own journey from bondage to freedom, from exile to restoration. The Psalms become vehicles for expressing our own laments, confession, and praise. As we enter in the stories of Jesus, we see ourselves and others through different eyes. Paul's life and witness opens new windows into the pilgrimage toward wholeness. Scripture locates our stories within God's story.

The doctrines of the church serve a similar purpose. Doctrine represents a set of foundational, theological beliefs agreed upon by the church and summarized in historic creedal statements such as the Nicene and Apostles' creeds. Theological exploration is the critical and constructive reflection on the doctrines and their appropriation in current or lived contexts.

A primal purpose of doctrine is that of providing a worldview, a lens through which to view the world.[4] The doctrines of the church provide a window into the transcendent dimensions of realities in which we live and move and have our existence. Science, for example, studies and describes the earth and works within the natural laws of the universe. The doctrine of God as Creator affirms that creation is brought into existence by God as an act of love and that "the earth is the LORD's, and all that is in it, the world, and those who live in it" (Ps 24:1). Therefore, viewing the world through the lens of God as Creator influences how we treat the world and live in it.

Viewing dementia through the doctrines of the Christian faith significantly broadens the perspective and influences how we see and treat people with cognitive degeneration. A central affirmation of Christian doctrine is the *imago Dei*, image of God. Such an affirmation challenges the notion that "we are our brains" and declares that human beings are more than their physiological components and capacities. We are creatures made in the image of God and have inherent worth and dignity. This is a theme to which we return in chapter 6.

Kinghorn warns of the danger of viewing persons with dementia only through a medical lens:

> Individuals and congregations that view persons with dementia primarily through the lens of sickness can inadvertently encourage them to view themselves as sick and defective, and primarily in need of technological cure within the medical system when what is needed, particularly in dementia's early stages, is a community capable of practicing hospitality and respecting dignity.[5]

Kinghorn helpfully adds:

> There is an appropriate and life-giving role for medicine and medication in the life of a person with dementia. Considered theologically, however, a person's status as a patient is always secondary, a social role rather than a defining identity. The corrective to the mistake that dementia is a disease of

the brain, and that a person with dementia is simply sick, is to emphasize that the person with dementia is primarily a wayfarer on a journey to God. Any social structure or practice of care, if it cannot reasonably answer the question, "What does this wayfarer need right now, in this context, for his or her journey to God?" is potentially dehumanizing, because it does not attend to the full account of what it means to be human.[6]

We are stories set within God's story of creation, liberation, restoration, incarnation, reconciliation, and transformation. Viewing dementia through the lens of theology helps to remove the stigma, enhances self-worth and dignity, fosters a sense of meaning amid the losses, provides a supportive community, and offers hope amid persistent grief and approaching death.

Theology beyond Cognition

Scripture, doctrines, and theological exploration involve memory, abstract and critical thinking, decisions, and actions of the will. What role, if any, do doctrine and theology play in the lives of those persons who have lost the capacity for recall, to think abstractly, and to make decisions? People with advanced cognitive disability can no longer read the Bible or recall its stories. The doctrines have disappeared from conscious thought; and the ability to make decisions and engage in liturgical practices has faded. Where is God within their reality of intellectual disability?

The Enlightenment with its elevation of reason and the Cartesian dictum, "I think, therefore I am," results in theology being limited to rational, intellectual engagement. Theology is the engagement of the brain! Thinking clearly, systematically, and coherently characterize theological discourse. The mind/body dualism confines God to the mind, the brain. The logical conclusion then is the degeneration of the brain means loss of God. The prevalence of such an Enlightenment notion results in neglecting the spiritual needs and theological gifts of people with dementia.

Pastoral theologian John Swinton writes and lectures extensively on dementia and theology. He identifies the danger of limiting theology to the cognitively able individual:

A good deal of theology...pivots on the assumption that the theologian is addressing an individuated, experiencing, cognitively able self, perceived as a reasoning, thinking, independent, decision-making being. This cognitively able self is assumed to have the potential to know and understand certain things about God—a God who is available at an intellectual level through such things as Scripture, revelation, prayer, or by means of some other form of communicable spiritual experience. Knowledge of God, sin, salvation, discipleship, sanctification, justification—they all tend to be assumed to relate to a fully cognizant being who can understand certain things, avoid or engage in certain activities and ways of thinking and who is able to make particular choices which have positive or negative implications and consequences for now and into eternity.[7]

Dementia challenges a theology that locates God exclusively or primarily in the confines of the human intellect and pushes toward a theology that transcends individualized cognition. Individuals live and think within communities, and autonomy apart from community does not exist. We are "storied" people; and our personal stories exist as part of the larger narratives of families, communities, and cultures. Christian theology affirms that we are baptized, incorporated into the story of God's life and mission and into the visible community (body) called the church.

Theology as Lived Reality

Theology is lived as well as thought. From a biblical and doctrinal perspective, human beings are more than their intellectual capacities. We are bodies endowed with God's breath, *nephesh*; and God's presence/spirit is not limited to our brains or cognition. As memory is both implicit and explicit, there is implicit and explicit theology. Implicit theology includes the embedded practices that have become integral to our living. This implicit theology is seen often in people with even advanced cognitive degeneration as bodily movements and gestures characterizing religious practices respond to stimuli.

What is at the core of the lived theology of those whose intellectual theology has been erased by disease? The question is especially relevant when religion gives priority to scholastic theology or defines faithfulness as "believing" the right things. Discovering and nurturing the lived theology of persons with dementia requires learning their stories and entering those stories with them. It requires attentiveness to their verbal and nonverbal expressions. And it means incorporating them into the ongoing life of the community where their stories and gifts are valued.

The implicit theology is evident in worship in the memory care facility. The worship experience begins as residents are brought into the worship space. The altar is prepared with paraments, a cross, and flowers. Many residents are milling around, some talking loudly. Yet, when the leader stands in front of the altar table, talking ceases and residents assume a posture of reverence. They represent a generation that values reverence in worship, and that communal component of their lived story remains.

I was part of a small covenant group several years ago that included a retired pastor who was in mid- to late-stage Alzheimer's disease. The group had been together for approximately fifteen years when I joined. For those fifteen years, the retired pastor had presided at Communion as the group concluded their weekly sessions. He now was unable to interact with the group other than simply being present. He sat silently for forty-five minutes, often asleep or with no apparent awareness of his surroundings. At the appropriate time, someone said, "Dick, it's time for Communion." Immediately, he opened his eyes and began, "The Lord be with you." There followed The Great Thanksgiving prayer,[8] which he led flawlessly.

Music and familiar Scripture reading frequently elicit visible bodily responses from those whose thinking and communication skills appear to be lost. Often the responses are nonverbal, the tapping of the foot, tears in the eyes, a smile, or look of joy in the eyes. Though the ideas or thoughts being expressed in the words of hymns, scripture, and prayers are beyond cognitive access, the feelings and movements associated may remain.

Dementia forces us to view theology as a lived, experienced reality. Theology is a way of feeling, seeing, loving, being! John Swinton states it clearly, "We need not only to know about God, we need to see God, to feel God and to love God in all things and at all times."[9] A challenge for those who journey with people with dementia is to recognize where God is present for and within those persons and to celebrate and rejoice in that presence.

Dementia as Theological Opportunity

Theology offers an alternative to the idolatry of rationalism and autonomy that dominate modernity and contribute to the dehumanizing and marginalizing of people with Alzheimer's disease and other forms of dementia. Entering the world of those with intellectual and other disabilities has the potential to transform our own experience and understanding of God and theology.

Regrettably, people with dementia are absent, thereby denying congregations the opportunity to grow in relationship and ministry with the God who is among the weakest and most vulnerable. As we shall discuss later, the church is oriented toward the intellectually and physically abled. People with disabilities, especially those with cognitive impairments, are hidden or relegated to the "homebound" list and are seen as objects of charitable ministry. Jean Vanier raises the crucial question: "Is it possible that people who are most rejected and pushed down are the ones who can teach us what it means to be human and lead us to peace?"[10]

People with Alzheimer's disease and other forms of dementia challenge the church to bear witness to God's power made perfect in weakness and to the enduring quality of love. They remind us that human identity lies in *being* as a beloved child of God rather than in our capacities.

Vanier's words are validated in my own experience as I journey with Linda and the residents of the memory care facility. They regularly lead me into the mysterious presence of God and deepen my understanding of what it means to be human. Here are some of the theological gifts I am receiving from accompanying people with dementia:

- God is present in the simple acts of giving and receiving love.

- We are more than our brains and intellectual capacity.

- Theology is lived more than thought.

- Basic tenets of the Christian faith broaden the lens through which we view dementia and travel with people with Alzheimer's disease and other forms of dementia: the nature and mission of God, incarnation, the *imago Dei* and identity, salvation, discipleship, source of hope, the nature and mission of the church, role of pastoral care.

Conclusion

Science is rapidly expanding the medical lens through which dementia is viewed. Knowledge and information about the brain and the diseases that threaten its health increase at a rapid pace as technology improves the means of identifying the complex structure and function of the brain. We celebrate the advances in medical research and support additional research.

Yet, dementia is more than a medical challenge. Neurocognitive disorders are bio-social-theological challenges and opportunities. Medicine with its continued focus on the body/soul dualism defines people with dementia in terms of symptoms and pathologies of the brain and central nervous system. Theology broadens the lens and sees people as stories within the context of God's story of creation and redemption.

Just as theology alters the way we view dementia and its impact, dementia pushes our theological boundaries beyond intellectual abstractions and systematic creedal declarations. We now turn to the interplay between key doctrinal/theological affirmations and dementia.

Chapter 4

Dementia and God's Nature and Action

Introduction

Students in the seminary class "Dementia and Pastoral Care" keep a journal of their encounters with residents at Bethany, the memory care facility on the campus of the Heritage at Lowman retirement community. A question to be reflected on is this: "Where did you see God in your encounter with residents today?"

A student was overheard remarking to a colleague on the first day, "What does God have to do with dementia?" From subsequent journal entries, the student's image of God and God's relationship to dementia significantly expanded as the result of relationships with Bethany residents. And his understanding of dementia was changed through his encounters with God.

The Bible, our historic creeds, the traditions of the church, the writings and lectures of scholars, the reservoir of hymns and liturgies, these have been and continue to be pathways into the mystery of God, a mystery deepened by the challenges of dementia. What if those pathways are blocked by diseases that expunge memories, jumble thinking, and erase language? What if one forgets God? Who and where is God to those whose intellectual disability renders the concept empty? What is God doing in the lives of those who have no cognitive grasp of God? Is God known exclusively or primarily through the intellect, or is God known beyond our neurological activities?

he answers these questions in this chapter.

Dementia challenges conventional notions about God centered in intellectual beliefs. At the same time, our understanding of the nature, presence, and action of God provides a lens through which to view dementia and its effects. Viewing dementia and its effects within the story of creation, liberation, and exile enables us to see our stories of chaos, bondage, and dislocation within the story of God's mighty acts of salvation.

The God Who Creates: Order from Chaos, Light from Darkness

Admittedly, Linda's diagnosis surfaced an age-old question: why? Medical research continues to probe the biological, chemical, and physiological answers to the causes of dementia. But our "why" has been a quest for meaning, purpose, and coherence when dementia seems meaningless, futile, and chaotic. One person lamented as he listened to his wife's incoherent babbling and watched her violently bang her fists against the wall, "How in the hell can a good God create or allow a disease that torments people like this? What has she done to deserve this?"

The stories of creation and "the fall," in Genesis 1–3 are theological lenses through which to consider God's action in relationship to the world, especially God's involvement in and response to human frailty, suffering, and imperfection. Two perspectives have dominated Christian tradition, and both have implications for how we view dementia's existence in God's good creation![1]

The prevalent interpretation in Western Christianity asserts that God created the world and everything in it as perfect, including human beings. The earth was originally flawless, harmonious, and pure. "The fall" resulted in the disordering, blemishing, and corruption of creation's goodness. Sinfulness and disobedience distorted and disfigured the divine image originally bestowed upon human beings. Banishment from paradise and the blighting of the whole creation resulted. Humans became mortal, and their entire nature was infected with sin. God's continuing action is the restoration of creation's original perfection, including the reshaping of human beings in the divine image.

In the Eastern Christian tradition, incompleteness and innocence characterized the original state of creation. God created and creates by bringing order from chaos, light from darkness, and maturity from innocence. Humans are created with the potential of reflecting the divine image and growing into the fullness of God's intention. However, wrong decisions and destructive actions thwart the fulfillment of God's intent for humanity and the whole creation. Creation is the arena for soul-making; and suffering, struggle, challenges, and death exist as opportunities for spiritual growth and maturity. God's presence and action are directed toward the healing, molding, reconciliation, and consummation of the divine dream for creation.

Does God create the diseases that result in dementia's symptoms? Reflecting a Western or Augustinian interpretation, John Swinton declares that since God is the sovereign creator of everything, God created dementia. He writes:

> It (dementia) is a mystery which is firmly rooted in God's creative and redemptive actions in and for the world. It may not be understandable. It may make us angry, distressed, and outraged. But it is not without meaning. In this sense, people with dementia are part of the flux of fallen humanity, but their condition does not alter their meaningfulness and their lovableness. . . . Despite the fallenness of our condition, everything we have and everyone we know exists because of God and is deeply loved by God.[2]

I find the emphasis on incompleteness and innocence in the Eastern, or Irenaean, perspective helpful when thinking of dementia and creation. Genesis opens with these words: "In the beginning when God created the heavens and the earth, the earth was a formless void and darkness covered the face of the deep, while a wind from God swept over the face of the waters" (1:1-2). The image is one of chaos and darkness; and God's creative action is in the form of bringing order from chaos and light from the darkness. There follows the emergence of conditions making possible life, beauty, and abundance.

Chaos and darkness are apt descriptions of what happens in the brain as cells and nerves die and connections become tangled. People who participate in "dementia simulation" exercises[3] frequently describe the experience as chaotic and disorienting. One person described the experience, "It feels like the world inside my head is going haywire and I'm being bombarded with thoughts and words I can't sort out." Thoughts and words are jumbled and incoherent. Vision and perception are distorted. Boundaries crumble, filters disintegrate, controls deteriorate, memories fade. Life feels chaotic!

Diseases resulting in dementia are examples of the unfinished nature of creation, and God continues to bring order from the chaos. Minimizing the disorder and disorientation are desirable goals of intervention. Forms of relaxation, meditation, and music are often effective means by which order is restored amid disorder. Anecdotal evidence and an increasing number of studies demonstrate that music is especially effective in fostering calm and orientation in people with dementia. I see it weekly in the memory care facility as order emerges amid chaos with the singing of familiar hymns. Even in the severe stage, Linda's movements and verbal expressions keep cadence with the music playing in the background. Perhaps the order, rhythm, and harmony of familiar music help put people with dementia in touch with the God-created harmony and order within creation itself.

Christian theology views the cosmos as an expression of God's love, which continues to work to heal, reconcile, and harmonize the often turbulent, chaotic creation. God's loving presence permeates the entire creation, and we are woven into the mysterious and intricate web of life (Ps 139). Metaphysical interpretations of the origin of suffering and disease are less important than the affirmation that a loving and creating God is aware of, and involved in, the totality of human experience, bringing order from chaos, light from darkness, harmony from dissonance, and life from death.

The God Who Liberates from Bondage

Memory care facilities are locked for the safety of residents. Occasionally someone manages to temporarily escape through an unsecured door. A woman raced through a side door while I was present. I ran after her and gently took her hand. As we walked back toward the entrance, I said,

"Jane (not her real name), come with me." With obvious agitation, she asked, "Where are you taking me? Back to that damn prison?"

A seventy-four-year-old North Carolina man pleaded guilty to voluntary manslaughter for killing his wife of more than fifty years. She had a form of dementia and was becoming increasingly difficult to care for in the home. The husband resisted admitting her to an assisted living facility. According to the investigating detective, "He felt like if he put his wife into the assisted living home that she would be like a caged animal."[4]

The seventeenth-century English poet Richard Lovelace wrote: *English Civil War 1648 +*

Stone walls do not a prison make,
Nor iron bars a cage;
Minds innocent and quiet take
That for a hermitage.[5] *a place of religious seclusion*

The imprisoned poet declares that the human mind cannot be locked behind stone walls or iron gates; freedom lodges in the intellectual and willful capacity to transcend physical confinement.

Alzheimer's disease and other forms of dementia, however, represent a different kind of imprisonment. The loss of mental, physical, and linguistic capacities and the absence of community participation eliminate or significantly diminish one's agency, autonomy, and volition. As one person in the early stage of Alzheimer's disease remarked, "I feel like I'm being imprisoned within my own diseased brain."

Surveys indicate that the elderly fear the loss of independence and being admitted to a nursing home more than they fear death.[6] Our culture highly values individual autonomy, self-sufficiency, and personal choice. The inability to exercise such values is viewed as a form of bondage or imprisonment.

Dementia involves growing dependency and decline in capability to care for basic needs. The ability to make simple decisions and perform minimal tasks diminishes, stripping away independence and freedom of choice and action. Many in the later stages, like my wife, Linda, become immobile and are confined to the bed, dependent upon others for all needs.

A core affirmation of Christian theology is freedom to flourish as God's beloved children and to participate in God's salvation of the whole creation. What does freedom mean when cognitive degeneration strips away individual agency, choices, language, and community? Where is God and what is God doing when human beings are in bondage?

The exodus story reveals God's relationship to those who are in bondage. According to Hebrew Scriptures, deliverance from Egyptian slavery is a pivotal event in the story of God's mighty acts of salvation. Even the stories of creation are viewed through God's liberating action among the Hebrew people. The God who set the captives free is the God who also creates and sustains the universe.

God's relationship with those in bondage is made known in the call of Moses as described in Exodus 3:7-8: "Then the LORD said, 'I have observed the misery of my people who are in Egypt; I have heard their cry on account of their taskmasters. Indeed, I know their sufferings, and I have come down to deliver them.'" God sees, hears, knows, and comes to deliver those in bondage!

The Hebrew word translated "know" is *yada*, which has a variety of meanings in Hebrew Scriptures, depending on the context. One scholar writes, "In the OT knowledge (*yada*) is experiential and relational."[7] It is more than intellectual information or cognitive awareness, and it most often denotes an intensive, experiential involvement "that exceeds a simple cognitive relationship."[8]

The word appears early in Genesis 4:1, "Now the man knew [*yada*] his wife Eve, and she conceived and bore Cain." In this context, *yada* is a deep, intimate, covenantal knowing that produces life!

Another helpful context is found in the wisdom book of Proverbs: "The righteous know (*yada*) the needs of their animals, but the mercy of the wicked is cruel" (12:10). The implication is that *yada* involves understanding the needs of those around us and showing mercy toward them, in contrast to the wicked who practice neglect and cruelty. To know is to identify the needs of others and to respond in mercy.

A third example of the meaning of *yada* in Hebrew Scripture is in prophetic literature:

Are you a king
    because you compete in cedar?
Did not your father eat and drink
    And do justice and righteousness?
    Then it was well with him.
He judged the cause of the poor and needy;
    then it was well.
Is not this to know me?
    says the LORD. (Jer 22:15-16)

To know (*yada*) involves more than intellectual awareness of the poor and needy, the vulnerable; it means to act justly on their behalf.

God the Creator is aware of, and intimately present with, those who are in bondage, ever generating life, mercy, and justice. To know God is to share in God's covenantal way of being and to practice solidarity, mercy, and justice on behalf of the captives, the poor, the needy.

Where is God, and what is God doing among those made captive by dementia? God is aware of, present with, showing mercy and compassion, seeking justice, and delivering them from the captivity and isolation of their diseases. As God called Moses, we are called to identify God's presence, participate in God's knowing (*yada*), and join in deliverance.

Expanding the meaning of "to know" is one means of deliverance. ✳ We are liberated from the enslaving concept that knowing is confined to intellectual awareness, stored information, and cognitive activity within the brain.

"Does Linda know you?" is a frequent question. I always have difficulty answering. She no longer recognizes me as her husband, and she doesn't recall our past together. She seldom can call my name. Yet, she knows me! The expression in her eyes, the occasional smile on her face, the slight squeeze of the hand—all communicate a knowing more profound than intellectual comprehension.

From my observation, many people with dementia know as God knows. They know with the heart what the brain cannot comprehend or process. Linda, for example, even in the advanced stage of her dementia, senses the moods of those around her and will sometimes ask, "What's wrong?"

Joining God's mighty acts of deliverance among people with dementia, moreover, involves identifying and nurturing the agency of those with dementia. The assumption that Alzheimer's and other forms of dementia destroy the ability to initiate action is wrong! Such an assumption leads to objectifying those with the diseases by reducing them to recipients of paternalistic charity or ministry. Their gifts are minimized or denied altogether. They are treated as objects of mission rather than participants in mission. Worship is done *for* them rather than *with* them. Instead of relating to them as a means of grace, they are seen only as recipients of grace.

Those living with the limitations accompanying neurocognitive degeneration may be means by which the liberating God frees us from our bondage to excessive reliance on our capacities as the source of identity and worth. Presence with them can free us to live creatively and joyfully in the moment, appreciating the simple experiences, and confirming that love is the enduring reality. We can be set free to know the God who sets the captives free.

The God Who Redeems Exile

Before Linda was admitted to the memory care facility, she persistently insisted on "going home," even though we were in our house. I often drove her around the neighborhood for a few minutes and upon returning announced, "We're home!" She would relax for a while, but soon she insisted, "I want to go home."

Frederick Buechner suggests that there is a longing within the human spirit for two homes—the home of our past where we first experienced life and love and the home of the future where worthy dreams of wholeness are fulfilled.[9] According to Buechner, we persistently live with "homesickness," as exiles in a strange land, remembering what has been but is no more and longing for a future home where we are restored, whole.

Buechner's description is especially appropriate for people in various stages of cognitive decline. "I want to go home" is a frequent comment from people in the memory care facility. "Who is at your home? Who

Where is "home" for us?

will you see there?" I now ask in response to the request. If the short-term memory has been erased, the person may be thinking of their childhood home and answer, "My momma and daddy." Or, perhaps they are thinking of the time when their own children were small and needed parental presence.

A frail ninety-six-year-old woman answered my question with one word, "Jesus!" She longed for her final home, "a house not made with hands, eternal in the heavens" (2 Cor 5:1). Upon entering Bethany two years earlier, she was restless and frightened. She wandered the corridors and courtyard, pleading to go home. Once she blurted out, "I feel like I've been dragged from my home and taken into exile." She subconsciously identified with the story of the Hebrew people and their captivity.

The Assyrian conquest of Israel in the eighth century BCE and Babylonian exile in the sixth century BCE were critical events in the history of the Hebrew people. Walter Brueggemann is among Old Testament scholars who contend that the exile shaped Jewish theology and practice and remains a fitting metaphor for the relationship of the church to prevailing culture.[10] The experience of exile led the Jewish people to reappropriate their tradition, rediscover their identity as the people of covenant, and envision a new future with hope.

In the sixth century BCE, Jerusalem was destroyed by Babylon's army, and the Jewish people lost their temple and their homeland. Many of the leaders, those with influence, were taken to Babylon. Those who remained were exiles in their own land. Life was forever changed as they were subject to Babylonian authorities and stripped of the center of their religious life—the temple where God's presence prevailed. Psalm 137:1-4 depicts the pathos of those living in exile.

By the rivers of Babylon—
   there we sat down and there we wept
     when we remembered Zion.
On the willows there
   we hung up our harps.
For there our captors
   asked us for songs,

and our tormentors asked for mirth, saying,
"Sing us one of the songs of Zion."
How could we sing the Lord's song
in a foreign [strange] land?

Indeed, exile is an appropriate metaphor for the reality of the dementia experience, especially those living in institutions. They are away from their homes, families, friends, familiar surroundings, and congregations. Their daily routines are determined by strangers who seldom know their life stories. People with whom they live behave strangely, speak incoherently, and unknowingly enter their private space. They are displaced, physically, emotionally, cognitively. D. Ps

Metaphorically, dementia itself puts persons in a strange and unfamiliar world. They are cut off from their past experiences, roles, recollections, and ways of relating. For many in the advanced stages of their symptoms, familiar people become strangers, sometimes even perceived enemies. Isolation increases as family members and friends visit less and less.

"Singing the Lord's song in a strange land" is a challenge for those cut off from "home." What insights into the nature and mission of God emerged from the Old Testament theology of exile, and how are those insights relevant for those who live in the strange land of dementia? How can people with dementia "sing the Lord's song" in dislocation, even when they forget their own identity and God?

Insights from the Exile

First, the ancient exiles learned experientially that God knows no exile. God's presence transcends all borders and is not confined to specific places, such as the temple in Jerusalem or the geography of Israel and Judah. The notion of the universality of the divine presence originated from exile. God lives in Babylon as surely as Jerusalem. God's sovereignty extends over all peoples and transcends all barriers, including the limitations of the human mind.

Poetry from the exile is replete with assurances that though the captives are displaced from their homeland and they may have forgotten God,
God has not forgotten or forsaken them:

> But now thus says the LORD,
>   he who created you, O Jacob,
>   he who formed you, O Israel:
> Do not fear, for I have redeemed you;
>   I have called you by name, you are mine. (Isa 43:1)

> Have you not known? Have you not heard?
>   The LORD is the everlasting God,
>   the Creator of the ends of the earth.
> He does not faint or grow weary;
>   his understanding is unsearchable.
> He gives power to the faint,
>   and strengthens the powerless. (Isa 40:28-29)

> The steadfast love of the LORD never ceases,
>   his mercies never come to an end;
> they are new every morning:
>   great is your faithfulness. (Lam 3:22-23)

God's steadfast, universal presence and love can be known (*yada*) experientially and relationally by those cut off from their past and living in
physical, emotional, and intellectual dislocation. Though they may have
forgotten God, God has not forgotten them; and in that affirmation lies
their identity, their worth, and their hope.[11]

A second theological influence of the exile experience is the recovery
of covenantal identity rooted in community and tradition. Old Testament
scholars document how the poets and prophets of the exile reinterpreted
and appropriated the traditions of creation, Abraham, and Moses. In so
doing, they enabled the displaced and dislocated people to recover and
maintain their compromised identity.[12]

When seen through the lens of exile, the rituals and laws of the tradition
as reflected in such writings as Leviticus are means of bodily remembering

Jewish identity and mission. They are actions that often transcend cognitive or intellectual comprehension. They are rituals of remembrance and identity, acts of knowing (*yada*) relationally and experientially. They are also experiences of order amid the chaos of dislocation.

The question of identity looms large for those with Alzheimer's and other forms of dementia and their families. A society that defines personhood by individual autonomy and capacities forces people with dementia into exile and potentially strips them of their identity. Exile theology provides a counternarrative that nurtures identity rooted in communal memories embodied in experiential practices that offer order amid chaos.

A third theological contribution emerging from exile is the language of lament. Individual and communal expressions of lament dominate the one hundred and fifty psalms, many specifically referencing the destruction of the exile. The book of Lamentations gives voice to the suffering, despair, grief, and longing of the Babylonian captivity. The laments strip away the denial, pretense, and escapist piety that often accompany suffering.

> My God, my God, why have you forsaken me?
>   Why are you so far from helping me,
>   from the words of my groaning?
> O my God, I cry by day, but you do not answer;
>   and by night, but find no rest. (Ps 22:1-2)

> How long, O LORD? Will you forget me forever?
>   How long will you hide your face from me?
> How long must I bear pain in my soul,
>   and have sorrow in my heart all day long?
> How long shall my enemy be exalted over me?
>   Consider and answer me, O LORD my God!
>   Give light to my eyes, or I will sleep the sleep of death. (Ps 13:1-3)

The poets of the exile knew that the first step in coping with suffering and loss is to acknowledge its ugliness and meaninglessness. Denial only compounds the destructiveness and slows the journey toward healing and peace. Laying the anger, despair, desolation, and weariness before the God of steadfast love is one avenue into God's healing presence.

During Linda's eighteen months of confinement in the memory care facility, the laments were my primary forms of prayer. They gave voice to my anguish at being separated from her and seeing her agony and confusion. Furthermore, I began to interpret her own expressions of agitation, frustrations, and resistance as her laments. The angry outbursts I came to view as prayers of lament to be accepted with patience and kindness.

A fourth theological concept emerging from the exile is that of "the suffering servant." Israel's understanding of its mission and God's way of being in the world progressed to encompass suffering, weakness, and vulnerability. The prophets interpreted the exile in the language of God's judgment upon their failure to fulfill their calling as a community of boundless compassion, generous justice, and inclusive hospitality. The exile confronted them with God's solidarity with the powerless, vulnerable, and dislocated; and it helped to shape Israel's understanding of their own mission to be among the powerless and vulnerable.

Isaiah 52:13–53:12 portrays God's "servant" as "a man of suffering and acquainted with (*yada*) infirmity; and as one from whom others hide their faces" (53:3). God's steadfast love and presence during exile transforms the suffering and dislocation into a redemptive, renewed, and reshaped community whose vulnerability becomes a means of God's salvation of the world.

Those exiled by Alzheimer's and other forms of dementia are contemporary "suffering servants" of God who know sorrow and illness and are those from whom others often hide their faces. Entering their world of dislocation and frailty is a pathway into the presence and steadfast love of the God who claims the vulnerable and despised as means of divine grace and transformation.

Finally, the image of exile provides hope for return! The final return from dementia's exile is eschatological in God's time; yet, there are intimations of the final restoration in the temporary times of remembrance, connection, and recognition. I daily experience intimations of Linda's ultimate return home in fleeting expressions of love, joy, and peace.

Chapter 4

Conclusion

The biblical/theological metaphors of creation, exodus, and exile provide a broader lens through which to view Alzheimer's and other forms of dementia than the strictly medical model with the focus on symptoms and deficiencies. Theology enables us to experience our stories within the greater story of God's mighty acts of creation, liberation, and restoration. The unfolding story of God's nature and action provides an alternative to the story of a mechanistic world in which human value lies in our cognitive capacities and individual autonomy. Within God's story is the invitation to participate in the very being and action of God who is known beyond the confines of the human brain.

Chapter 5
Dementia and the God Who Is Incarnate

Introduction

"She's moving to another world, Ken," remarked a longtime friend and experienced hospice chaplain, Karl Netting. He added, "Being present in her world is hard and sometimes impossible; but your presence in her world is important for both of you. There will come a time when you will have to let go and give her permission to enter a totally new world, but accompanying her as far as you can will bring you both sorrow and joy."

Those wise and compassionate words have become a guiding principle for my relationships with people who navigate the mysterious world of dementia. Linda's world is filled with confusion, agitation, combativeness, apathy, sadness, and withdrawal. The temptation is to avoid her world, *all of us!* argue with it, deny it, resist it, escape it.

How does one enter a world composed of chaotic thought processes, sporadic comprehension, and jumbled language? Medical researchers and practitioners search for ways of intervening in the disordered world of dementia. Thus far, the intervention is largely in the form of pharmaceuticals designed to relieve or diminish adverse symptoms.

Facilities created in response to dementia predominantly reflect the medical approach to Alzheimer's and other forms of dementia. They are most often units or hallways attached to skilled nursing facilities and under the supervision of nurses and other medical personnel. They provide a secure, controlled environment with activities appropriate for the residents. Such facilities become an alternative world where those with dementia live in community under the supervision and attention of medically trained personnel.

During the eighteen months that Linda lived in the specialized facility, I moved in and out of two worlds; and she fearfully inhabited a strange new environment. Being present with her was a persistent challenge filled with grief and frustrations as I attempted to get inside her realities and those of other residents. In so doing, I encountered anew the Incarnate God who brings creation into being, sets the prisoners free, and visits those who "mourn in lonely exile."

Incarnation: God for and with Us

Dementia clouds all thoughts about God and shatters all theological constructs. Stories of God's revelation and acts of salvation fade from memory. Language of the creeds and affirmations of God's presence in creation and in the experiences of bondage and exile evaporate into the fog of cognitive decline. The concept of God often becomes nothing more than what one person called "a vague, oblong blur."

I find great comfort and assurance in the affirmation that God knows our suffering and loss and that God is present to create, heal, comfort, and sustain us. Yet, what that means to Linda remains unknown. Is there a limit to God's identification and solidarity with Linda as she forgets everything she has intellectually, consciously known about God?

I have learned much about dementia from my observation and attempts to understand Linda. Learning about the brain and the latest research continues to be helpful. My observations and attempts to get inside her world continue to teach and guide me. Yet, I can't get fully inside her world and experience her realities. I can love her, comfort her, care for her; but an impenetrable wall exists between us, a chasm that cannot totally be bridged.

At the heart of the Christian tradition is the incarnation, the Word made flesh. It's a radical declaration that the Creator of the infinite universe, with all its complexity and mystery, has become vulnerable flesh in

Jesus of Nazareth and shares in the frailty and dependency of the human condition. But does that mean that God's knowledge of dementia is experiential or only detached observant awareness?

What does incarnation mean for those who live in the world of dementia? How does God know that world experientially and relationally? We know that Jesus as the Incarnate Word experienced suffering, grief, loneliness, frustration, anger, rejection, abandonment, and death. But dementia—lost intellectual capacity, forgotten past, inability to communicate?

John's Gospel declares:

> In the beginning was the Word, and the Word was with God, and the Word was God. . . . All things came into being through him, and without him not one thing came into being. . . . And the Word became flesh and lived among us, and we have seen his glory, the glory as of a father's only son, full of grace and truth. (John 1:1, 3, 14)

The Greek concept of *logos* (word) has a long, wide-ranging philosophical and theological history with rich implications for God's relationship with creation, including people who live with dementia. In Greek, *logos* includes language and the thoughts behind language, words and the reality preceding the words. For Greek philosophers, the term denotes the organizing principle controlling the universe. Human reason or intellect is a small-scale facsimile of the cosmic logos.

Logos is related to the Hebrew concept of wisdom. "The intelligible element in God's mysterious being; the means of God's self-disclosure to the world; the source of its rational order."[1] Logos as wisdom formed creation and sustains and guides the ongoing life of the universe. The Hebrew word for wisdom is *hokmah* and alternately *chokhmah*. When the Hebrew Scripture was translated into Greek between the third and second centuries BCE (the Septuagint), the Greek word used for wisdom was *sophia*. The image of wisdom in Hebrew Scripture is personified, especially in the Septuagint. For example, Proverbs 1:20 reads, "Wisdom cries out in the street; in the squares she raises her voice."

The opening verses of John's Gospel weave the various linguistic, theological, and philosophical threads of logos/word/wisdom into the tapestry of what Christian theologians, since the fourth century, have referred to as the incarnation. The very essence at the foundation of all that is has become flesh in a human being, Jesus of Nazareth. The eternal God who brings creation into existence, liberates from bondage, and restores from exile "became flesh and dwelt among us, full of grace and truth."

The Word that in the beginning was "with God" and "was God" has now "become flesh" and "dwelt among us."[2] Gail R. O'Day writes, "The relationship between divine and human is transformed, because in the incarnation human beings are given intimate, palpable, corporeal access to the cosmic reality of God."[3]

God is more than an intellectual construct or cognitive abstraction. God is known, experienced within the flesh and blood of human existence. God chooses "to live with humanity in the midst of human weakness, confusion, and pain.... To become flesh is to know joy, pain, suffering, and loss. It is to love, to grieve, and someday die. The incarnation binds Jesus to the 'everydayness' of human experience."[4] God enters human existence in all its frailty and vulnerability!

God's incarnation is not limited to Jesus's cerebral cortex and hippocampus. God entered the entirety of the human flesh, claiming every cell, organ, and function as pathways of divine presence. God is, therefore, present and experienced in all that constitutes a human person. The senses—sight, taste, smell, hearing, and touch—are receptors and expressions of God's own being. God's presence and activity within human beings transcend human consciousness and cognition.

Incarnation takes on added significance when considering people with cognitive impairments. A consequence of enlightenment's prioritization of reason and the Cartesian dualism, popular understandings of theology rely almost exclusively on mental capacity. Confining God to the intellect runs counter to the holistic understanding of what it means to be human as well as who and where God is.

God's incarnation in Jesus the Christ did not begin with Jesus's public ministry. Jesus's total existence is the Word made flesh. Jesus was the Word made flesh as a whimpering, dependent child with a soiled diaper as surely as an adult presenting himself for baptism at the Jordan. He was no less the incarnation of God while nursing at Mary's breast than while caring for her in his dying moments. He was the Son of God while carving wood in Nazareth and while being nailed to a wooden cross on Golgotha.

During those obscure years in Nazareth, Jesus was simply present with his family, friends, and neighbors. We know nothing of what he did for those around him, only that he "increased in wisdom and in years, and in divine and human favor" (Luke 2:52). His very presence redeems and transforms.

Sam Wells suggests that *with* is the most significant word in the Christian faith. Jesus is God both for us and Emmanuel, God with us. Jesus was the incarnation of God during the obscure years in Nazareth and in his three years of public ministry. Wells writes, "If Jesus was all about working for, how come he spent 90% being with (in Nazareth), 99% working with (in Galilee)—and only 1% working for (in Jerusalem)."[5] Jesus is about being *with* as well as being *for* us.

Western Christendom has tended to prioritize the cross as the lone saving act while minimizing the redemptive significance of Jesus's life. While the cross bears witness to the depth of God's saving presence, the drama of the crucifixion is inseparable from the redemptive significance of the ordinariness of Jesus's life in Nazareth. God's entrance into the commonplaceness of human existence infuses the simple, unspectacular, obscure, and routine with promise and purpose.

Incarnation and Redemption

The redemptive power of the incarnation lies in God's entering humanity's dependency, helplessness, frailty, and death. God is radically with us. Sam Wells makes a helpful distinction between being for and being with.[6] The Bible is the story of God's mighty acts of salvation, stories of what God does for us. His public ministry is viewed as God doing for humanity. His teachings, miracles, and supremely his death and resurrection are expressions of God for us.

We will explore the meaning of personhood in the next chapter; however, it is important to affirm that incarnation, God's assuming human flesh, did not end with Jesus of Nazareth. The triune God has taken up residence in our being and relationships. We are extensions of the incarnation! God is for and with us in our confusion, weakness, frailty, suffering, and death.

Where is the Word made flesh in those whose cognitive abilities are being destroyed by diseases? How do they experience the divine presence when their mind cannot comprehend? Since God is incarnate in the totality of human personhood, the body is "a temple of the Holy Spirit" (1 Cor 6:19). Therefore, we experience God's presence in our bodily senses; and people with diminished cognitive functioning maintain sensory capacities, and some capacities are heightened as the disease progresses.

Gentle touches, glimpses of beauty, sounds of music, the fragrance of fresh flowers, the taste of familiar food—these become expressions of the Word made flesh within the experience of people with dementia. Abstract thoughts vanish and words disappear, but God's incarnate presence remains.

Incarnation as Paradigm for Relationships

example/pattern

Incarnation bears witness to the nature, presence, and purposes of God; and incarnation is the paradigm for our being with one another. As God in Jesus Christ enters humanity's confused, broken, and vulnerable world, so we are invited to enter the world of others in their confusion, ordinariness, brokenness, and vulnerability. In entering their world, we encounter the Word made flesh.

People with Alzheimer's and other forms of dementia bear within their own existence God's grace-filled presence, and they are means of the divine presence to those who choose to be with them. Since much of our interpersonal exchanges depend upon intellectual and language capacities, relating to people with dementia is particularly challenging. Relating to people with dementia requires a deeper understanding of what *with* means. The incarnation provides that deeper understanding and grounds our presence with one another in God's presence with humanity.

In his book *Incarnational Mission: Being with the Church*, Sam Wells identifies eight components of "being with" that are derivative of the Word made flesh: presence, attentiveness, mystery, delight, participation, partnership, enjoyment, and glory.[7] I will deal with four of these components as an avenue into the world of those with the symptoms of dementia.

1. First, to *be with* requires physical presence. While this seems self-evident, isolation and loneliness are common to the elderly in general and even more so among those with dementia. A growing population in America is what some call "elder orphans," unmarried and childless persons over the age of sixty-five. According to one study, 25 percent of those over sixty-five are currently or are at risk to become "elder orphans."[8] These vulnerable elders are also at greater risk to develop the symptoms of dementia.

Dementia often results in a different isolation, the isolation resulting from disconnectedness from the people around them. Some of the isolation is self-imposed as people with dementia withdraw from social contact as their cognitive and language capacities diminish. Fear of saying the wrong thing, acting inappropriately, or being unable to keep up with conversations often lead people in the early to mid-stage of their diseases to avoid being with others.

While nursing homes and memory care facilities play an important role in elder care, they too often are warehouses of loneliness. One study found that up to 60 percent of nursing home residents have no regular visits from the outside.[9] The author of the study postulates that the percentage is much higher for those with dementia. From my observation over four years of chaplaincy in a memory care facility, the residents who have at least weekly visits from the outside are the exception.

A major contributing factor to the isolation of people with dementia is fear and discomfort on the part of family members and pastors. "She doesn't recognize me when I visit, and she forgets I was there, so why visit?" is a common statement. Or, "He just stares at me and I can't communicate with him, so there's no point in my going." So, the result is intensified isolation. John Swinton poignantly states that the tragedy isn't that people with dementia forget; it is that they are forgotten.[10]

Therefore, the first requirement for "being with" is to be in the presence of people with dementia. Indeed, "Presence proclaims value; it says to those with advanced dementia: 'You are still important. You are still my mother, grandfather, fellow member of the body of Christ, neighbor. You still have a great deal to give me. You are still a human being.'"[11] As God in Christ is present with humanity, thereby declaring our worth and dignity, so we are present with one another as a declaration of the worth and dignity of the other.

2. "Being with" also involves disciplined attentiveness. A recurring theme in the Bible is God's persistent attentiveness to human existence. As the psalmist declared:

> O LORD, you have searched me and known me.
> You know when I sit down and when I rise up;
>   you discern my thoughts from far away.
> You search out my path and my lying down,
>   and are acquainted with all my ways.
> Even before a word is on my tongue,
> O LORD, you know it completely. (139:1-4)

Jesus declared that even the hairs of our head do not escape God's attention and that a lamb cannot wander unnoticed from the fold. Jesus was attentive to the touch of his garment by a woman seeking healing, and he heard the concern of a Roman soldier for a sick daughter. Even in his dying hour, he was attentive to a plea from a convicted criminal and to the future of his grieving mother.

Astute attention must be paid to those with dementia! Such attention begins by honoring their inherent worth and dignity, and it requires consideration of their sensitivities and ways of communicating. Many people with dementia are hypersensitive to nonverbal communications, voice tone, and touch. Communication with them requires familiarity with and attentiveness to their individualized mannerisms, expressions, and feelings.

Such attentiveness is emotionally intensive and entails time and energy. In our fast-moving and task-oriented world, few people take the time to be truly attentive. Often staff members in institutions have insufficient time and energy to be attentive to the individualized qualities of those for whom they care. The attentiveness needed to truly be with necessitates the "self-emptying" of one's own agenda and preoccupation and requires focus on the unique person in whose presence they sit.

3. A third component of being with is mystery. Mystery is at the core of the incarnation! It is impossible to rationally exhaust the meaning of the Word made flesh or to explain the constituent components of the identity of Jesus the Christ. The church points to the inherent mystery in the incarnation with such creedal statements as "human and divine" or as the Nicene Creed states: "We believe in the one Lord, Jesus Christ, the only Son of God, eternally begotten of the Father, God from God, Light from Light, true God from true God, begotten, not made, of one Being with the Father." Now, that is mystery!

While Christians affirm Jesus the Christ as the ultimate and unique incarnation of God, every person's existence is enveloped in mystery. We cannot be reduced to our biological and intellectual components and capacities. Every person is an ineffable mystery to be approached with a degree of reverence and awe. Openness to the wonder and inexplicable in the other avoids reducing one another to our physical, behavioral, and intellectual characteristics.

Mystery is the appropriate place to begin when relating to people with dementia. Such an approach "sees the extensive disability and profound irreversible, advancing illness as a mystery and not as a problem. It doesn't treat them as fundamentally needy, miserable, or pitiable. It doesn't define people by what they're not."[12] We approach them, not as problems to be fixed or symptoms to explain and control; rather, they are people whose lives are to be entered, celebrated, explored, and appreciated.

My journey with Linda over the last decade has deepened my own sense of mystery inherent in each person. While I try to understand the underlying causes of her behavior and ways of interacting, I can never fully comprehend. When I least expect it, there is a fleeting moment of connection, an unexpected sparkle in the eyes, a new gesture, an outburst of laughter, an indication of a recovered memory. Being with her is to live in the presence of an ever-unfolding mystery to be welcomed, loved, and celebrated.

4. Another dimension of "being with" is delight in the other. Dementia is accompanied by the persistent stripping away of capacities, and the tendency is to focus exclusively on the resulting deficits rather than on gifts that frequently surface unexpectedly. Some capacities recede; others emerge. A friend whose husband is in mid-stage of Alzheimer's disease shares his childlike delight in simple things—jet stream in the blue sky, a small insect crawling on his shirt, a cone of ice cream that is new each time he eats it. Additionally, prior to the onset of his disease, he tended to be rather cynical in his view of humanity and current events; however, the disease seems to have dissolved the cynicism and enhanced a sense of delight and humor.

Conclusion

Part of the delight in being with people living with Alzheimer's and other forms of dementia is what they bring out in us. I'm a different person for having been with Linda and other people with cognitive degeneration. Yes, there are times of great frustration, sadness, and anguish; but those are countered by a profound deepening and expansion of love without reciprocity. The delight in the simplest expressions of life, love, and joy is heightened. Patience grows as limitations are accepted. As Mary's love, compassion, patience, and gratitude were called forth by the mere presence of her son, so Linda's very presence prompts me to be a more loving and whole person. The incarnation pushes us toward a deeper understanding of what it means to be a person, the subject to which we now turn.

Chapter 6

Dementia and the Meaning of Personhood

Introduction

"She's not the person she used to be," remarked the nurse practitioner after announcing that Linda had scored zero on the Mini Mental State Examination (MMSE).[1] I got the distinct impression that she didn't consider Linda a person at all. She never looked at her or acknowledged that she was sitting across the table. A zero on a standardized cognitive exam apparently rendered her a nonperson.

My friend's wife was confined to the bed for almost a decade as dementia erased her memories and reduced her capacities to basic bodily functions. She lay in an apparent comatose state for months. My friend visited her three times each day, insisting that she was still aware of his presence. Many who had known her now considered her a "vegetable" rather than a person and stayed away. Not her husband! He said, "She's still a person; she's my wife!"

"I'm not a person! I'm just stupid!" Those are the words of a former American Baptist pastor and mental health chaplain, an avid reader with two master's degrees and an expansive vocabulary. Once supremely self-confident and articulate, he currently can speak few words and often feels that he is no longer "a person."

People with dementia confront an identity crisis. In a society that defines human identity in terms of individual capacities and autonomy, decline in brain functioning means diminished self and lost personhood.

Who am I if I have no recall of my past and have even forgotten my name or can't recognize myself in the mirror?

This perceived loss of self has enormous consequences for those with dementia and the ones who care for them. It partly accounts for their isolation and neglect by society and the loss of a sense of worth and dignity by those with dementia. Further, the loss of a sense of self-worth likely contributes to the exceptionally high suicide rate among the elderly.[2]

Competing Anthropologies

Neuroscientists, psychologists, physicians, philosophers, and theologians are raising anew old questions about the essence of personhood: Who am I? What constitutes the self? What does it mean to be a person? The Judeo-Christian tradition offers a wider lens than human capacities and individual autonomy as the essence of identity.

The essence of what it means to be human has occupied attention throughout history. The psalmist's question echoes across the centuries: "When I look at your heavens, the work of your fingers, the moon and the stars that you have established; what are human beings that you are mindful of them, mortals that you care for them?" (Ps 8:3-4).

Cartesian Dualism and Materialism

The Enlightenment, with its accent on reason and rationality, heightened the quest for an answer to that age-old question. René Descartes (1596–1650), French mathematician, philosopher, and scientist, is considered the father of modern philosophy. His philosophy was built on the foundational notion that "I exist," and the intellectual consciousness of existence is a distinctive human quality. From that emerged his most famous quote, "I think, therefore I am."

Descartes contended that there are two components of human identity: mind (mental) and body. The material body cannot think in and of itself, and the mental, or mind, exists outside the body. This conceptualization gave rise to widespread mind/body dualism, which is expressed in the theological notion that the soul inhabits the body but exists apart from it.

This mind/body dualism provides rationale for the materialist view that the body is a complex machine with multiple interdependent parts, and the immortal soul lives temporarily within the body. Medicine, in such a view, deals with the body in similar fashion as an auto mechanic approaches a motor vehicle or an electrician deals with circuits. Medical specialization potentially intensifies the dualistic tendency, especially if the focus on one organ of the body is at the expense of the whole person.

During a seminar with nurses, certified nursing assistants (CNAs), and others who care for people with dementia, I emphasized the importance of treating people with dementia kindly, sensitively, compassionately, and with dignity. A staff supervisor stated that the most important thing is skill and keeping their bodies clean and safe. While affirming the importance of safety and skill, I suggested, "More than technical skill is necessary. People with dementia are more than bodies with a diseased brain; they are persons with inherent worth, longings, and spiritual needs." The supervisor implied that mind/body dichotomy and assumed that medicine deals with the body while someone else deals with the soul.

The prevalence of mind/body dualism in relation to people with dementia is expressed in such destructive attitudes as "She's only a shell of a person" or "He's just not there anymore" or "I lost her years before she died" or "There's no use visiting her; she's no longer there." And, it is prevalent in institutions with overworked, poorly trained, and minimally supported staff who meet basic bodily needs, thereby reducing the persons to a collection of symptoms without stories.

Capacity-Based Identity

Much of human identity in Western culture is capacity based—I am what I know, think, and produce. Philosophers such as Descartes and John Locke (1632–1704) defined a person by their capacities, with the cognitive attributes of critical thinking and continuity of memory as essential qualities. The logical conclusion of these philosopher's theories is that the decline in rational thinking and cognitive recall renders the person with dementia a nonperson. Persons are stripped of their essence as humans and become at best "a shell" of a person or a body without a mind/soul. Such notions of personhood can become rationales for euthanasia, assisted suicide, or isolation and neglect of those whose cognitive capacities have been destroyed by Alzheimer's and other forms of dementia.

The British philosopher Anthony Quinton (1925–2010) proposed criteria for personhood that starkly reflects the capacity-based perspective. He listed five entities as essential components of "person": consciousness of self, rationality, agency, morality, and the capacity to form and maintain relationship.[3] Dan W. Brock, an American bioethicist and Harvard professor emeritus, states his view of what it means to be a person as follows:

> Personhood is incompatible with the complete absence of any present and future capacity for purposive agency, social interaction, or conscious experience of any sort whatever. Human beings who have suffered this tragic loss lack even the capacities for pleasure or pain, and for goal-directed action or behavior, of animals that are controversially held to lack the capacities for personhood.[4]

As one critic stated, "By establishing criteria by which to exclude a human from the realm of personhood, we have designed and iced a slippery slope."[5]

Individualism and Autonomy

Stanley Hauerwas provides a caution regarding the use of the concept of "person." In an article entitled "Must a Patient Be a Person to Be a Patient? Or, My Uncle Charlie Is Not a Person but He Is Still My Uncle Charlie," he argues that referring to others as a person relegates them to an abstraction, severing them from their community and their story.[6] Personhood cannot be reduced to individualized physical and cognitive attributes isolated from social structures and unique narratives or stories.

Individualism and personal autonomy are additional philosophical components of a capacity-based notion of personhood. American culture highly values individualism and tends to define personhood as an independent, autonomous self, with the capacity to initiate, act, and control. The words of the poet William Ernest Henley are a prevalent mantra:

> It matters not how strait the gate,
> How charged with punishments the scroll,
> I am the master of my fate,
> I am the captain of my soul.[7]

The diseases that cause cognitive degeneration progressively alter the sense of self, the capacity to consciously initiate action and to relate to others. Some people reach the stage of forgetting their names and faces as well as their entire past. The ability to consciously determine actions diminishes and boundaries of behavioral control cease. In the severe stage, all visible forms of interaction may cease with minimal or no reciprocal interaction with others.

Without capacity for critical thinking, language, agency, and reciprocal interaction, who am I? Am I a full human being? Where does my identity lie when I have forgotten who I am? A broader lens than the Cartesian dualism, the individual autonomy, and capacity-based perspectives is needed for people with dementia to be considered fully human and persons with worth and dignity.

Toward a Broader View of Human Identity and Personhood

Many theorists have challenged the notion that people with dementia become sub- or non-persons. Thomas Kitwood (1937–98) reconceptualized personhood by not linking it exclusively to cognitive functioning. He contended that personhood is sacred and unique and that *being* in-itself is enough criteria. He defined personhood as "a standing or status bestowed upon one human being by others in the context of particular social relationships and institutional arrangement. It implies recognition, respect and trust."[8]

Personhood, then, has an element of transcendence or sacredness and is bestowed by others. Kitwood challenged the prevailing biomedical view of dementia by postulating that the person is more than a disease, which is only one aspect of their lives. To be a person is to have intrinsic value as a unique human being with personal stories and relationships, thereby worthy of respect and dignity.

His academic training as a social psychologist contributed to Kitwood's emphasis that personhood is "a product of relationships with others and can be nurtured or diminished, depending on whether the person is being valued or depersonalized."[9] Kitwood theorized that "malignant social psychology" that stigmatizes, objectifies, or ignores the person with dementia contributes to the loss of a sense of personhood and contributes to decline.[10]

Kitwood was influenced significantly by the Jewish existential philosopher Martin Buber (1878–1965) and his concept of "I-Thou" versus "I-It" as the essence of all relationships. In his book *I and Thou*,[11] Buber argues that we engage with the world as an I-Thou, with reverence, respect, and full acceptance of the totality of the other; or we relate to the world as an I-It, which treats the other as an object that is understandable, manageable, and conquered or controlled. I-Thou is a relationship of subject-to-subject, while I-It is a relationship of subject-to-object.

Both Kitwood and Buber view persons as sacred expressions of the "eternal Thou" and, therefore, should be related to as whole persons, not simply in terms of specific isolated qualities or characteristics. I-Thou relationships are characterized by mutuality, respect, and reciprocity. I-It relationships, on the other hand, are characterized by detachment, separateness, and utility.

Many contemporary theorists build on the work of Kitwood and Buber as they emphasize the relational nature of personhood. A common theme among these scholars and theorists is the notion "that people are involved in a web of personal and social relationships which constitute a large part of their personhood."[12]

As noted previously, the language of personhood has its limitations; and postulating relationships as an essential component of personhood raises similar concerns. Such a concern is noted by pastoral theologian John Swinton. While acknowledging the contribution of Buber and

Kitwood in moving beyond capacities, Swinton cautions against defining the essence of personhood relationally. Kitwood has established that relationships themselves are essential to being a person. What if no such relationships exists? Swinton writes: "The problem is that if it is our relationships that make up our personhood, then presumably if we don't have such relationships, we are no longer persons."[13]

Who am I? I am more than a collection of cells, molecules, and organs that function mechanistically within a self-contained body. I am more than my capacities to think, to initiate action, to produce, and to relate. I am a complex being with intrinsic value wrapped in a web of interpersonal and social relationships with a personal history and story that is part of a larger societal and cultural narrative. But theologically, I am even more! I am part of the transcendent story of God's mighty acts of creation, redemption, and transformation.

Personhood through a Theological Lens

Buber's I-Thou and Kitwood's relational-centered understanding of personhood were profoundly influenced by their theological perspectives. Theology significantly expands what it means to be a person, and that perspective is especially relevant when considering people with disabilities and those with dementia particularly. The Judeo-Christian tradition offers a distinctive anthropology that counters the dominant mechanistic, materialistic, individualistic, capacity-valued way of defining what it means to be human.

Christians and Jews affirm that the essence of human identity is derived from God who brings creation into being and gives it life. As poetically described in Genesis 1–2, God fashioned human beings from the dust of the earth and breathed into them the breath of life: "Then the LORD God formed man from the dust of the ground, and breathed into his nostrils the breath of life [*nephesh*]; and the man became a living being" (2:7).

The Hebrew word *nephesh* is often translated "soul," which has been interpreted by some Christian theologians as supportive of the Cartesian dualism of body and soul (mind). However, other theologians such as

what if you are neither Christian nor Jewish?

Thomas Aquinas (1225–74) never interpreted the soul as separate from the body. "For Aquinas…a human being is not a soul that temporarily inhabits a body (and who is said to be 'gone' when the body becomes disabled or demented), but rather a living, ensouled body, a body that carries personal identity and spiritual significance."[14] Human beings, then, are ensouled bodies created by God whose identity is bestowed as a gift independent of capacities or personal agency.

The *Imago Dei*

God not only gave life to these earth-creatures called Adam (man) and Eve (woman) but also created them in the divine image, the *imago Dei*: "So God created humankind in his image, in the image of God he created them; male and female he created them" (Gen 1:27).

What constitutes this "image of God" has been debated over the centuries and some interpretations contribute to the dehumanizing of people with dementia and other forms of disability. A commonly held notion emerging from the Enlightenment is that the image of God is lodged in the intellect, the ability to think, reason, and cognitively recall and integrate thoughts.

Fortunately, many theologians counter the destructive notion that the image of God lies in the intellect and other capacities. Martin Luther (1483–1546) provided a blunt rebuttal to such a notion:

> If these powers (memory, will, and mind) are the image of God, it will also follow that Satan was created according to the image of God, since he surely has natural endowments, such as memory and a very superior intellect and most determined will to a far higher degree than we have them.[15]

Although theologians differ as to what constitutes the *imago Dei*, the consensus is that it is bestowed by God as a gift. It is not self-created or achieved. It includes the potential to reflect qualities of God and sharing in God's life and being.

Influenced by both Eastern and Western Christianity, John Wesley (1703–91) contended that God's prevenient, or "preventing," grace is universally present in and with all people and prevents the destruction of the divine image.

Christians affirm that Jesus the Christ is the ultimate fulfillment and embodiment of the *imago Dei* and the means by which that image is restored in us. In the incarnation, God hallowed human existence and endowed personhood with sacredness, even in its most vulnerable, frail, and dependent condition.

The Apostle Paul, schooled in both Greek philosophy with its glorification of human agency and capacity and in Jewish theology of creation, considered Jesus Christ as the revelation of personhood and the status of human beings. In her book *Paul and the Person: Reframing Paul's Anthropology*, New Testament scholar Susan Eastman summarizes the significance of Christ in defining personhood as follows:

> Paul's anthropology counters any criterialism about qualifications for being a person, precisely because it is grounded in the story of Christ's mimetic assimilation to the human condition. Paul's "master story" about what is most deeply true about human beings is not, in the first instance, the creation narrative but the story of Jesus Christ: his being sent into the world in the likeness of the flesh of sin, his identification with sinful humanity to the point of death, and his victorious resurrection from the dead. This socially embodied divine action grants dignity and worth to every human being—that is, to every creature whose "form" Christ assumed.[16]

Christian theology affirms that in baptism we are incorporated into Christ's life, death, and resurrection; therefore, our identity lies in Christ. The declaration from the heavens at Jesus's baptism declares who Jesus is and who we are through Christ: "You are my Son, the Beloved; with you I am well pleased" (Mark 1:11). God in Christ bestows, defines, secures, and fulfills our identity as a gift; and that identity is received, celebrated, and nurtured in community.

Drawing upon an image and insights from Thomas Aquinas, physician and theologian Warren Kinghorn identifies humans as "ensouled bodies" created by God, imbued with the desire for God, and who are on a grace-filled journey toward God. We are "wayfarers on the way to God." Kinghorn writes:

In creation and in grace, through the person and work of Christ, God invites this body [ensouled body] to be drawn into God's life.... This living, ensouled body is beckoned by desire on a journey toward God, and aided in that journey by the grace mediated in creation and in the sacraments. Under the conditions of a broken and sinful world ... this body will inevitably encounter internal and external obstacles to the journey, including disease, finitude, and even death. However, God continues to claim and to draw this finite body, even if she bears the particular finitude of dementia, into God's infinite love.... It is always this body who is sacred, this body who is being drawn to God, this body who will be raised and transformed in Christ for eternal life in the presence of God.[17]

John Swinton helps to shift the focus from the definition of personhood to God's own nature and action in relationship to human beings. It is God who creates, sustains, empowers, and transforms all existence. It is the same God who creates us, knows us, and remembers us. Being held in God's memory is the essence of our identity and destiny. And such an identity is unrelated to our capacities. Swinton declares: "'I think, therefore I am' is replaced with 'We are because God sustains us in God's memory.' Our hope lies in the fact that we are living in the memories of God. As long as God remembers us, who we are will remain: 'I will not forget you. See, I have engraved you on the palms of my hands'" (Isa 49:15-16).[18]

how big is your god.

Conclusion

"I know you miss her," remarked an acquaintance upon learning that Linda has dementia. "Oh, she's still with me," I responded, assuming she had misunderstood my statement to mean that Linda had died. An awkward pause followed. "Yes, but I assume Linda isn't the same person she used to be. My mother had Alzheimer's. She lived for almost ten years after the diagnosis, but she was only a shadow of her true self for the last four years. We felt we lost her long before the end came."

Such comments express a definite reality: dementia strips away many personal qualities and capacities by which a person has been known and experienced. In a capacity-dependent definition of what it means to be a person, people in the severe stages of dementia cease to be persons. They, thereby, lose worth, dignity, relationships, and even a legitimate claim to compassionate recognition and care. But such a view has to be challenged!

Neuroscientists, psychologists, philosophers, ethicists, and theologians are increasingly challenging the capacity-dependent and mind/body materialistic definition of what it means to be a human being. The question "Who am I?" is being complexified and expanded; and the Judeo-Christian theological tradition significantly contributes to broaden the lens to include ALL people, including those with severe mental, physical, and emotional degeneration and disintegration.

Dietrich Bonhoeffer's poignant poem captures the essence of the Christian response to the question "Who am I?"

Who am I? They mock me, these lonely questions of mine.
Whoever I am, Thou knowest, O God, I am thine![19]

Chapter 7

Dementia and the Meaning and Source of Salvation

Introduction

Upon learning of Linda's diagnosis, a friend asked, "Ken, I have put Linda on my daily prayer list. How shall I pray for her and you?"

That's my persistent question as Linda goes through the stages of her dementia. My frequent prayer is, "God, I don't know how to pray. I want Linda healed of her confusion; but if that isn't possible, I want the best for her. I just don't know what that is!"

"I don't know what is happening to Mom! She's never cursed in her life and now every word is profanity; and she used to be so sweet and kind. Now she is just plain mean and hateful! She has been religious all her life, but it doesn't seem to mean anything now!" These are the expressions of a daughter concerned about the spiritual well-being of her mother who is in late stage of frontotemporal dementia.

A man diagnosed with Lewy body disease asks, "Why is this happening to me? It's not fair. I've led a good life and haven't done anything to deserve this. Where is God, Reverend? I've prayed for God to heal me, but I only get worse! I'm not only losing my mind; I'm losing my faith!"

"I'm not sure my husband is saved. He has been a good man, but he never made a profession of faith or went to church. Now he doesn't understand anything I say about God or Jesus. He just stares at me with that blank look on his face." She is a member of a faith community that defines *salvation* as involving conscious intellectual assent and willful commitment to <u>prescribed beliefs and practices</u>. Her husband's Alzheimer's disease has eliminated his grasp of abstract concepts, severely limited his language, and abolished volition. Added to the wife's intense grief is concern for her husband's "salvation."

At the core of the Christian faith is soteriology, the doctrine(s) of salvation. What is the relationship between soteriology and dementia? What is the telos or overarching goal of "God's mighty acts of salvation"? What is the relationship between health and salvation? What is the relationship between individual salvation and community? These are among the questions to which we now turn.

What Is Salvation?

Salvation is the <u>underlying theme of the Bible</u> and the Judeo-Christian tradition. The various words for salvation indicate its comprehensive nature. Two major salvific terms in Hebrew are *ga'al* ("<u>redeem</u>," "<u>buy back</u>," "restore," "deliver," or "<u>set free</u>") and *yasha* or *yesha* ("save," "help in time of distress," "rescue," "deliver," or "set free").[1] The New Testament word *sōzō* ("save," "<u>heal</u>," or "liberate") and the corresponding nouns *soteria* ("salvation"), *soter* ("savior"), and *soterion* ("salvation"). Many other terms are used in the New Testament to express salvation, including "freedom," "justification," "life," "<u>reconciliation</u>," "redemption," and "resurrection."[2]

While the biblical terms for *salvation* are comprehensive, Christian interpretations and emphases have evolved over the centuries, and its meaning varies across the theological spectrum. For some, forgiveness of sins and reconciliation with God define the essence of salvation. A personal decision and conscious commitment to Jesus as "Lord and Savior" constitutes salvation for many. Salvation involves believing and behaving in identifiable and prescribed ways, with the goal of "going to heaven."

These aspects of salvation are especially prominent in Western Christianity with its emphasis on human sinfulness and God's initiative in pardoning individuals, thereby restoring proper relationship with God. While various interpretations of God's action in Jesus Christ regarding salvation have developed across the centuries, <u>the central affirmation is that through Christ's life, death, and resurrection, God pardons and reconciles</u>

[handwritten margin note:] which word feels right to you?

sinful humanity. Repenting of our sin, accepting God's forgiveness, and devoting our lives to following Jesus's teaching and example through the power of the Holy Spirit are the components of salvation.

Individualism plays a significant role in the interpretation of salvation, especially in Western Christianity. The focus is on individuals and their personal beliefs, decisions, actions, and relationships. Salvation is interpreted as something that happens within the individual's experience and requires personal initiative and agency.

The Cartesian body/soul dualism coupled with individual autonomy resulted in a narrowing of salvation as having to do with the soul of individual persons. As stated previously, medicine had to do with the body while religion was relegated to the soul. Salvation, then, consisted of "saving souls" and freeing the soul from the body.

Eastern Christianity's emphases related to salvation tend to be more toward healing as a dominant metaphor. The interpretation of the fall in Genesis 1–3 is less on the loss of original perfection and more on original innocence and the necessity of continual growth and the healing of brokenness. Salvation is growth toward the fullness of God's image in which humans are created. Forgiveness of sin is an important element in the healing of the human condition and the growth toward the fullness of God's image; however, healing is more comprehensive and inclusive than simply the pardoning of sin.

John Wesley, the eighteenth-century Anglican priest and founder of Methodism, was significantly influenced by both the Eastern and Western Christian theological perspectives. His treatises and sermons include the language of pardon as well as healing in speaking of salvation. The following represents his definition of salvation:

> By salvation I mean, not barely (according to the vulgar notion) deliverance from hell, or going to heaven, but a present deliverance from sin, a restoration of the soul to its primitive health, its original purity; a recovery of the divine nature; the renewal of our souls after the image of God in righteousness and true holiness, in justice, mercy, and truth.[3]

Wesley writes to a friend in 1778, "It will be a double blessing if you give yourself up to the Great Physician, that He may heal soul and body together. And unquestionably this is His design. He wants to give you...both inward and outward health."[4]

Viewed from the broad perspective of Christian theological traditions, salvation is the healing, reconciliation, restoration, and transformation of individuals, communities, and the entire creation. It is creation in all its forms flourishing in accordance with God's intention. This comprehensive view of salvation is described in many memorable biblical images:

> The wolf shall live with the lamb,
>> the leopard shall lie down with the kid,
> the calf and the lion and the fatling together,
>> and a little child shall lead them.
> The cow and the bear shall graze,
>> their young shall lie down together;
>> and the lion shall eat straw like the ox.
> The nursing child shall play over the hole of the asp,
>> and the weaned child shall put its hand on the adder's den.
> They will not hurt or destroy
>> on all my holy mountain;
> for the earth will be full of the knowledge of the LORD
>> as waters cover the sea. (Isa 11:6-9)

> Your steadfast love, O LORD, extends to the heavens,
>> your faithfulness to the clouds.
> Your righteousness is like the mighty mountains,
>> your judgments are like the great deep;
>> you save humans and animals alike, O LORD. (Ps 36:5-6)

> See, the home of God is among mortals.
> He will dwell with them;
> they will be his peoples,
> and God himself will be with them;
> he will wipe every tear from their eyes.
> Death will be no more;

mourning and crying and pain will be no more,
for the first things have passed away. (Rev 21:3-4)

While these express the eschatological vision of God's salvation, they poetically move the boundaries beyond what we often label as "personal salvation." They push us to envision a holistic understanding that includes the total person's wholeness and well-being—physical, emotional, intellectual, spiritual, and relational.

This broader understanding is especially important when considering people with dementia. What does holistic salvation mean for people with dementia? Is salvation only a futuristic, eschatological hope; or can people with dementia experience reconciliation, healing, and wholeness in the present?

Salvation and Human Agency

Intellectual assent to prescribed doctrines and willful commitment to a set of practices are deemed critical components of salvation. Yet, the diseases that cause dementia render those components impossible. Those, such as my wife, who once "believed" the doctrines and participated in the practices forget basic beliefs and lose the ability to choose participation in once-practiced rituals and behaviors. Do they, thereby, lose their salvation? Or, do those who never were part of religious beliefs and practices have limited, if any, ability to intellectually accept beliefs or learn new practices? Does that cut them off from salvation?

Who is the primary agency in salvation? While Christian theology declares that God is the agency in salvation, there is also an emphasis on human initiative and response. The prominent biblical text reads, "For by grace you have been saved through faith, and this is not of your own doing; it is the gift of God—not the result of works, so that no one may boast" (Eph 2:8-9). Grace is defined primarily as "undeserved gift" and salvation, therefore, is bestowed as God's gift.

Yet, willful response is an expected component, or for some interpreters, a required response. Faith may be defined as "trust" that enables one to accept God's gift. One must raise the question, however: If trust is a

willful response to God's gift, is an intellectual, cognitive rejoinder necessary? Again, persons with dementia may not have the capacity to willfully
trust or consciously accept God's gift.

An expanded understanding of grace is helpful. Rather than grace being something God bestows as a wrapped gift to another person, grace is
God! Wherever God is, there is grace! God's grace is the gift of God's presence and power to create, reconcile, and transform individuals, communities, and the entire creation. Grace is universally present and persistently
active to bring healing and wholeness to the whole creation.

Responding to God's presence and power isn't limited to, or dependent upon, intellectual capacities. Our hyper-valued cognitive capacities
and excessive individualism tend to lodge salvation in personal agency and
having correct beliefs. However, few of our responses and actions result
from conscious intellectual decisions. Our actions and feelings emerge
from multiple stimuli, most of which are unconscious and are shaped
by varied forces beyond our individual, cognitive awareness. Feelings and
actions generated from exposure to sensual expressions transcend self-
conscious thoughts; and those expressions are authentic responses to God's
grace as surely as the verbal declarations of the church's creeds.

Salvation as Communal/Relational

The dominant emphasis on individualism prevalent in much of Christianity minimizes the communal/relational components of salvation.
However, the biblical emphasis is clearly on the wholeness of the community; and as indicated in a previous chapter, the Bible has no concept
of individual autonomy existing apart from community. God's salvation
is the creation, reconciliation, and transformation of the nation or the
community.

The Bible is the story of God's creation, deliverance, forgiveness,
reconciliation, and restoration of "a people." The Psalms are filled with
prayers that God will continue to deliver God's people (Pss 28:8-9; 60:5;
108:6; 33:19). The expansiveness of God's salvation for all people is evident in many passages, especially in Isaiah and Second Isaiah (Isa 2:1-4;
49:6, 22-23; 60:1-14).[5]

Like the Hebrew Scriptures, the New Testament highlights the general and collective rather than the individual human condition that makes people candidates for salvation. While individuals within the community are both candidates for and recipients of God's saving acts, the focus is on the creation and sustaining of communities of reconciliation.

The Apostle Paul's letters are written to and for congregations. To the community in Ephesus, he writes, "For by grace you have been saved through faith, and this is not your own doing; it is the gift of God—not the result of works...so that no one may boast" (Eph 2:8-9). It is the community that receives and embodies God's presence and power to create, reconcile, forgive, and transform; and it is in community that individuals are formed and sustained in God's saving grace.

The doctrine of justification's communal dimension is often overlooked, thereby distorting the fullness of God's salvation. Justification includes incorporation into community as well as personal forgiveness and pardon.[6] Through baptism we are incorporated into God's covenantal community, which affirms our identity as beloved children of God, receives us as members of the household of God, and commissions us to participate in God's salvific mission.

Individual wholeness and well-being, therefore, cannot be separated from the wholeness and health of the community. Salvation of one is inextricably bound to the salvation of the community. This is crucial in considering the implications of salvation for people with cognitive impairments. As previously stated, dementia cannot be limited to a disease of an individual's brain.[7] Consequently, the healing, reconciliation, and wholeness that characterize wholistic salvation require attentiveness to the dysfunctions and brokenness within the broader community.

Much of the suffering of people living with Alzheimer's and other forms of dementia results from social stigma, isolation, and lack of knowledge and advocacy by the broader community, including the church. There is growing evidence to indicate that quality, loving, and skilled care positively affect the progression of the symptoms and the quality of life of those with dementia. In other words, the community affects the ways in which persons with dementia experience wholeness, health, and healing.

Mediating God's Salvation

While God is the primary agency in salvation, the community and individuals serve as mediators. Self-salvation is not a biblical perspective; deliverance comes through God's action usually mediated through human actors. Through Moses, God delivered the Hebrew slaves from Egyptian bondage. Through the prophets, God prepared the exiles for restoration and set them free through a "pagan" Persian king, Cyrus.

Mary was called as one to give birth to the Messiah, and John the Baptist "prepared the way of the Lord." Jesus is the supreme Mediator of God's wholistic salvation, but he enlisted others to share in his acts of healing, forgiveness, reconciliation, and transformation. Mary and Martha provided hospitality to Jesus at their home in Bethany (Luke 10:40f). Ananias of Damascus became an agent of healing and comfort for Saul during his blindness following his encounter with the risen Christ (Acts 9:13-19).

The Apostle Paul declared: "All this is from God, who reconciled us to himself through Christ, and has given us the ministry of reconciliation; that is, in Christ God was reconciling the world to himself... and entrusting the message of reconciliation to us" (2 Cor 5:18-19). The community and its members are agents of God's salvation! Paul refers to the Christian community as "the body of Christ" with each part of the body contributing to the ministry of the whole (1 Cor 12:27).

Again, the implications for people with dementia are clear. The healing, reconciliation, and wholeness of the people living with dementia require the mediation of the community. The presence and attentiveness of the community is essential for the wholeness to be experienced by those with dementia and their families. To help people with dementia experience quality of life amid their limitations, persons who enter their worlds with compassion and kindness embody God's salvation.

The medical community plays a significant role in the healing and wholeness of people with dementia. Medications and treatments of diseases that underlie and control the symptoms are expressions of salvation as is the research into causes and remedies. Skilled and compassionate physicians, nurses, certified nursing assistants, and other professional caregivers are means of God's healing presence. Advocacy groups such as the Alzheimer's Association provide prophetic voices on behalf of justice, compassion, and aid for those without voice.

Families, neighbors, friends, and congregations are indispensable mediators of God's salvation to those living with dementia. The most devastating tragedy is that people with dementia tend to become isolated from such loved ones. Such isolation diminishes and even thwarts participation in God's salvific action for both the person with dementia and their community.

A seldom acknowledged reality is that those with dementia are mediators of God's salvation to us. As stated in previous chapters, God has chosen the weak, the vulnerable, the powerless as preferential recipients and means of God's grace-filled action. Jean Vanier speaks poignantly of those who chose to be present with the disabled and distressed:

> People who gather to live in the presence of Jesus among people in distress are therefore called not just to do things for them, or to see them as objects of charity, but rather to receive them as a source of life and of communion. These people come together not just to liberate those in need, but also to be liberated by them; not just to heal their wounds, but to be healed by them; not just to evangelize them, but to be evangelized by them.[8]

A daughter shared with her Orthodox priest her reluctance to care for her frail mother with dementia. The priest responded, "But your salvation may depend on your care for her; she may very well be the means to your salvation."

Mediation of God's salvation requires entering solidarity and presence with the other, as God has entered solidarity with humanity in Jesus Christ. John Swinton tells the story of a student in his class who was hearing impaired. She told of a dream in which she was with Jesus. "He was everything I hoped he would be," she said. "And his signing was beautiful!"[9] What meant the most to her was not Jesus healing her of her impairment. Rather, it was Jesus's solidarity with her.

This is not to imply that we earn our salvation by our service to the vulnerable and the powerless. Rather, it is the recognition that we encounter the living God in those with whom God in Christ is in solidarity and we are thereby changed. I can affirm without equivocation that Linda has been and continues to be a means of my own reconciliation, healing, and wholeness. Through my relationship with her, my ability to love without reciprocity has grown, my patience has increased, my attentiveness in the moment has intensified, my celebration of the simple things has amplified, my priorities have changed, and my faith in the indestructibility of love has fortified. And, I am experiencing that salvation is both a present reality and a future hope!

Salvation within and beyond Time

The healing, reconciliation, and transformation of individuals, communities, and creation is a process. Creation is always evolving. Healing is partial and limited. Reconciliation remains unfinished. Transformation is incomplete. We live in between God's vision of the new heaven and the new earth and the world as it now is, between God's present reign brought near in Jesus Christ and God's final reign in the new heaven and the new earth.

God's salvation has the character of already but not yet. The healing, reconciliation, and transformation we experience in the present is an intimation of the eschatological wholeness and transformation envisioned. We live now within the finiteness, frailties, and limitations of human existence, and salvation occurs within those limitations.

We are creatures who inhabit space and time and we are humans who value the ability to live in the past through memory, inhabit the present with agency, and anticipate the future with hope. As we have stated, some contend that it is the ability to live in those three dimensions of time that make us human. But dementia shatters such a notion! People with advanced dementia live in the present moment, without a consciousness of a past or a future. What does salvation as perceived in time and space mean to those to whom only the present is real?

God isn't confined to time and space; and the past, present, and future do not define God's time. Building on the insights of St. Augustine, John Swinton affirms: "Time is not an impersonal, free-floating commodity intended for the satiation of human desire. It is an aspect of God's relationship with the world, a gift from the loving Creator. Time is best conceived as an aspect of God's love for the world. As an aspect of God's love, the purpose of time is to facilitate and sustain love."[10]

While God's salvation is cosmic and eternal, it is also expressed within space and time. Each moment of time is a gift of God and occupied with God's timeless presence. God's presence is filled with grace, which we have defined as the power to create, heal, reconcile, and transform. Each moment contains potential for manifestation and mediation of God's salvation by facilitating and sustaining love.

The consequences for people who live with dementia are enormous. People who live only in the moment live within God's salvific presence and power. To generate and nourish love is to participate in God's salvation, and each moment is occasion for sharing in God's love that creates, reconciles, and transforms.

Jolene Brackey leads popular seminars for caregivers. Her book, *Creating Moments of Joy*, and her lectures are filled with practical ways of generating moments of joy by being attentive to the stories of people with dementia.[11] Rather than focusing on joy as a permanently sustained mood, Brackey concentrates on the experiences that trigger brief, fleeting expressions of connection, love, and joy. Those temporary and short-lived moments have residual and long-lasting benefit for both the person with dementia and the ones who care for them.

Linda has reached the stage where only the present moment is real. She seems to be aware of presence only when I appear in her line of vision or she hears my voice or experiences my touch. Often, my appearance will elicit a fleeting smile, a flashing twinkle in the eye, or a subdued laugh. As I entered her room after she awoke on a recent morning, she spotted me and said with unexpected coherence, "I love seeing you!" I responded, "I love seeing you, and I love you. You're my sweetheart." With joyful laughter, she retorted, "You're a mess!" Then, as quickly as the connection had emerged, it was gone, and she lapsed into incoherent chatter and drifted off to sleep. But in a moment, love was facilitated and shared; and we were both enriched.

The nurse practitioner who supervises Linda's care visits our home every two months. She has provided medical care for Linda for the last four years and has witnessed the progression of her symptoms. While in the memory care facility, Linda lost twenty-five pounds and reached the point of being unable to walk or feed herself. She was evaluated by her physician and the hospice physician, both of whom declared her eligible for hospice care. When I asked for an estimate of her longevity, the consensus was up to a year.

During the nurse practitioner's visit twenty-eight months later, the same nurse looked at me and said, "This is amazing. I would never have thought she would still be with us; and she seems at peace." "What do you think accounts for her being with us and at peace?" I asked. She replied, "She's been loved to life!" I responded, "And so have I!"

Conclusion

From the day of Linda's diagnosis, I have longed for her healing. I would like nothing more than to have all her cognitive capacities and personality traits of earlier years restored. I want her to be whole! I have prayed for her deliverance from the bondage of disease, to be restored from the loneliness of her exile, and to be re-membered as part of the Christian community. I want her to share in God's salvation and for her to be a mediator of salvation to others.

My images and experiences of God's salvation have expanded and deepened as the result of the journey with people affected by dementia. These steadfast convictions have emerged or been confirmed:

- Salvation is holistic and includes healing, reconciliation, forgiveness, and transformation of human beings, communities, nations, and the entire cosmos.

- God is the primary agency for salvation, not human capacities, including intellectual beliefs.

- Individual/personal and social/relational salvation are inseparable; each person's wholeness is tied up in the wholeness of the community.

- Individuals and communities are mediators of God's salvation.

- Salvation is both "already" and "not yet."
- God's timeless salvation is experienced within God's gift of time and the purpose of each moment is to facilitate and nurture love.

People with dementia are both recipients and mediators of God's mighty acts of salvation.

Chapter 8
Dementia and Christian Discipleship

Introduction

"Who is Jesus?" asked a woman during worship when we announced that we were going to sing "Jesus Loves Me." She was a lifelong member of the church and had taught hundreds of Sunday school children about Jesus and had sung the hymn regularly in our worship services. Now, the syllables *Je-sus* meant nothing to her.

Each week I lead worship with thirty to forty people, most of whom are in the mid-stages of diseases that impair their thinking and communication. Most of them have been participants in churches for six or seven decades. They have known the creeds, participated in the rituals and liturgies, and faithfully attempted to fulfill their baptismal and membership vows to support the church. They have exhibited the marks of Christian discipleship.

Now, many of the observable components of Christian discipleship have disappeared from their daily lives. Church participation has fallen by the wayside. Creeds have been erased from their understanding. For some, Jesus and God are meaningless concepts. Even behavior boundaries have weakened, and a straight-laced pastor now uses profanity and a deaconess makes indiscriminate sexual overtures.

A pastor and chaplain with Alzheimer's disease laments, "I'm not any good to anybody! I can't do anything anymore!" His lifelong vocation as an ordained pastor and counselor of the mentally ill has been relinquished as he becomes increasingly dependent on the aid of others. He is but one of many whose Christian discipleship and vocation seem to be in peril as their intellectual and language capacities fade.

Congregations largely view people with dementia as recipients of ministries rather than as participants in ministries. They are objects of mission, not contributors to mission. Once seen as persons with gifts contributing to the health of the congregation, they now are relegated to the "inactive roll" with no expectations to contribute. They become invisible!

Are people with dementia only emeriti Christian disciples? Can they follow a Jesus whom they have forgotten? Do they have a Christian vocation, a calling? How can their discipleship and vocation be nurtured and their gifts celebrated and utilized in service to the church's mission? These are among the issues meriting continuing reflection.

The Meaning of Christian Discipleship

A class of seminary students listed the following in response to the question, "What does it mean to be a Christian disciple?"

- To believe in the Apostles' and Nicene creeds
- To accept Jesus as Lord and Savior
- To follow Jesus
- To share in Christ's ministry in the world
- To love God and neighbor
- To participate in the life and mission of the church
- To trust in God's mighty acts of salvation, supremely in Jesus Christ
- To surrender one's whole being to God's grace and will

"Can a person in the advanced stages of Alzheimer's or another form of dementia meet these criteria or components?" the professor asked. A long silence ensued before a student responded, "I think so, but it makes me question what it really means to be a Christian disciple. All of these imply intellectual understanding and personal, conscious action or decision."

John Swinton writes, "Dementia does not affect discipleship or humanness; it reveals 'hidden' aspects of both."[1] Viewing discipleship through the lens of dementia uncovers the "hidden" aspects of discipleship and counters the exclusion of people with dementia from the company of Christian disciples.

A disciple is defined as a "follower," "student," or "apprentice" of a mentor. Jesus is called "rabbi," or teacher, and his disciples learn about and from him. The church's Christian education enterprise endeavors to teach and form people as disciples of Jesus Christ. Theological education as practiced in recent decades prioritizes intellectual understanding and adept articulation of the doctrines, history, and interpretations of the Christian tradition.

Intellectual knowledge, theological astuteness, and communication are essential components of Christian discipleship. Christian discipleship, however, involves formation as well as information. Being precedes doing and believing. It is estimated that 5 percent or less of what we do results from conscious cognitive reflection. A researcher in cognitive psychophysiology affirms, "An enormous portion of cognitive activity is nonconscious, figuratively speaking, it could be 99 percent; we probably will never know precisely how much is outside awareness."[2] While our conscious intellectual beliefs affect our actions, our actions also impact our beliefs.

Who we are and how we act is largely pre-cognitive. That is, much of our formation occurs unconsciously and results from interaction with the world around us. We are formed by relationships, experiences, practices, and interaction within community. Our being is formed by a complex of stimuli, experiences, and relationships prior to any conscious cognitive reflection, recollection, or knowledge accumulation. We are being formed by the ethos, or prevailing spirit, and character of the culture of our community. Christian formation is "caught" as well as "taught."

As one pastoral theologian affirms, "Christian learning begins before we think about it and, by implication, it continues after we have ceased to think about it."[3] Another writes, "[Christian education] is a holistic endeavor that involves the whole person, including our bodies, in a process of formation that aims our desires, primes our imagination, and orients us to the world—all before we ever start thinking about it."[4]

As we have discussed in previous chapters, the mind, from a Christian perspective, is a way of imagining, orienting, and being in the world. Memory is more comprehensive than the recollection of events, relationships, beliefs, and intellectual reflections. We are embodied memory, and our memory is formed by practices, experiences, and relationships of which we are cognitively unaware. The "mind...that was in Christ Jesus" (Phil 2:5), which characterizes Christian disciples, is birthed, nurtured, and expressed in the totality of our being as we exist in community.

People with dementia, even in severe stages, embody behaviors and responses that reflect the orientation, imagination, and way of being that exceeds their cognitive awareness. I see it regularly in Linda and among the people in the memory care facility. The embedded practices emerge in activities, unexpected insights, and responses. They know in mysterious ways that defy mere intellectual explanation.

The experience of Helen Keller is instructive. From about age two, she lived without sight and hearing and, therefore, was locked in a world of darkness and silence. She learned, however, to communicate through touch. Her teacher, Anne Sullivan, traced letters on the palms of her hand. Miss Sullivan introduced Helen to the famed preacher Phillips Brooks. With Miss Sullivan translating, the eloquent preacher told her about God who loved her and who came among humanity in Jesus Christ. As the words entered her through the gentle touch of Anne Sullivan, Helen smiled and said, "Mr. Brooks, I always knew he was there; I just didn't know his name."[5]

The reality of which Jesus is the incarnation cannot be confined to the language of prescribed creeds or the intellectual grasp of abstract thoughts. Love in all its varied components is the fundamental reality embodied in Jesus the Christ and those designated as Christian disciples. Love is not an abstract thought; it is a way of being that is formed in relationships and experiences. It is expressed in the intricate and complex web of our total existence and the conscious and unconscious dynamic of giving and receiving love.

John Swinton refers to the Apostle Paul's image of disciples as "letters" written by Jesus on human hearts:[6]

> You yourselves are our letter, written on our hearts, to be known and read by all; and you show that you are a letter of Christ, prepared by us, written not with ink but with the Spirit of the living God not on tablets of stone but on tablets of human heart. Such is the confidence that we have through Christ toward God. (2 Cor 3:2-4)

The heart is considered in Hebraic anthropology to be the governing center of human identity and existence; or, as Swinton writes, it is "the seat of the entire person."[7] So, when Paul considers Christian disciples a "letter from Christ" written "with the Spirit of the living God," he is declaring that our whole personhood bears witness to the living God.

All this is to say that dementia does not threaten or diminish Christian discipleship. On the contrary, dementia forces us to broaden the scope of discipleship beyond abstract beliefs, intellectual formulation and reflections, and prescribed behavioral activities. Christian discipleship is a way of being that bears witness to and engages with the reality of divine presence and love.

The Dance of Love: Essence of Christian Discipleship

Both Hebrew Scriptures and the New Testament declare love for God and neighbor as the summary of God's expectations and goal for humanity. At the heart of Jewish daily prayer is the Shema based on the command in Deuteronomy 6:4-5: "Hear, O Israel: The LORD is our God, the LORD alone. You shall love the LORD your God with all your heart, and with all your soul, and with all your might." The prayer begins and ends the day, declaring that the goal is that one's whole existence (heart, soul, body) be formed in divine love.

When asked to identify the greatest commandment, Jesus responded with the Shema, "You shall love the Lord your God with all your heart, and with all your soul, and with all your mind." Then he added a commandment from Leviticus 19:18b, "You shall love your neighbor as yourself" (Matt 22:37-39). Jesus not only taught about love but also was the incarnation of divine love. Love permeated his whole being and flowed freely in all his relationships and actions. His final commandment to his disciples is this: "Love one another as I have loved you" (John 15:12).

The Apostle Paul declared that love is the ultimate gift and surpasses all other capacities, including knowledge and language (1 Cor 13). Love endures when all else ceases! Nothing in all creation, including dementia, can separate us from God's love (Rom 8:38-39). First John states it succinctly and clearly, "God is love, and those who abide in love abide in God, and God abides in them" (4:16b).

The love at the core of discipleship is characterized by identification and solidarity with the other in shared vulnerability and mutual longing. It is connecting at the deepest level of common identity as beloved children of God. Love is covenantal commitment to seek the well-being of the other with patience, humility, kindness, and perseverance.

Such love consists of and is nurtured in practices of devotion, self-giving service, and generosity. It is more than a sentiment; it is acts of comfort, forgiveness, healing, justice, and advocacy. Love is also the willingness to receive, openness to the gifts of others, acceptance of dependency, and acknowledgement of limitations. Such evidences of love are not limited to the cognitively abled; people with dementia also embody love's qualities and actions.

The essence of Christian discipleship is this: participation in the giving and receiving of love. Theologically, it is the love defined in the intimate relationship within the triune God, which is characterized by a dynamic dance of creating, redeeming, and sustaining. The dance moves with the unfolding drama of life's transitions and challenges, always giving and receiving, holding on and letting go. Participants in love's dance are bound together in a covenant of faithfulness and devotion grounded in God's steadfast love.

Participation in the triune God's dance of love is not dependent upon human capacities. Through the Holy Spirit, we have been choreographed into God's dance in creation and in the life, death, and resurrection of Jesus Christ. At the dawn of creation, God breathed into human flesh resonance with God's own spirit (*nephesh*), and in Jesus Christ, God claimed humanity as recipients and mediators of God's grace-filled presence. Deep within every person is the latent and/or active capacity to share in divine love.

Christian discipleship, then, consists of our participation in the triune God's dance of love, whatever our status or capacity. We are part of God's drama, or dance, of love! Identifying and fulfilling our part in that dance is the essence of Christian discipleship. Our specific roles change as circumstances and contexts demand. Sometimes we take the "lead" in the dance; other times we are dependent. At times, we may perform "solo"; or during other occasions, we may passively receive the gifts of others.

Dementia does not remove persons from participating in the triune God's dance of love! On the contrary, they represent some of the most inspiring and challenging occasions for exercising the essence of discipleship. From my observations over the last decade of living with and relating to people with dementia, I have yet to meet anyone who failed to respond to love! Some of the most profound demonstrations of divine love have come from people with dementia, even in the severe stages.

Linda no longer remembers Jesus or comprehends basic doctrines or participates in acts of piety and mercy. Yet, she is no less a Christian disciple than when she taught Sunday school, led training events, joined in corporate worship, served "meals on wheels," and shared in mission projects among the poor. While her role in the dance of love has changed, it is no less significant or valuable in the drama of God's love. Her role is largely that of receiving the expressions of love from those around her.

As Linda receives my love, expressed in simple acts of cleaning her teeth, caressing her face, holding her hand, or brushing her hair, my love expands and together we release into the world more of God's infinite love. Or, in the metaphor of the dance, we expand the triune God's dance of love; for in God's dance, "no act of love is ever wasted."[8] The caregivers who skillfully, tenderly, and patiently care for another's basic needs join the dance. The neighbors who stop in daily to lend support and the couple from church who bring a meal each week widen the circle. And the dance goes on! We all grow in discipleship!

Sometimes the acts of love are reciprocated with visible responses—a whispered "thank you," a fleeting smile, a twinkle in the eyes, or a sigh of relaxation amid agitation. At other times, there is no visible response, no reciprocal expression of love. The temptation may be to assume that our acts of love don't really matter. "After all, she doesn't even know I'm here!" But if our love is a participation in God's love, the full response is beyond the visible or measurable. We love by faith; that is, we trust that deep within the beloved and in God's economy, the love makes a difference.

The caregiver's discipleship amid dementia is often challenging. The dance is difficult when one participant resists or stumbles or insists on running away. Symptoms of Alzheimer's and other forms of dementia frequently appear as the opposite of Christian discipleship—anger, hostility, violence, apathy, expressions of hate and disdain. Our expressions of love may not be received with generosity or gratitude.

Our discipleship in such difficult times may be reframed by reminding ourselves that the difficult behaviors are manifestations of the underlying disease rather than intentional responses to us. Withdrawing temporarily can be the most loving act, or providing a distraction, or letting another assist. Discipleship, when sharing in the dance of love, requires a lot of improvisation, discipline, and patience. But, when viewed as a participation in the triune God's dance of love, discipleship grows.

Discipleship as Communal

It is important to note that discipleship involves community. It is the community that engages in the dance of the triune God. The call to discipleship is a call to be part of a community that embodies love for God and neighbor. The triune God's dance of love is a communal dance of mutual support, giving and receiving, leading and following. The Apostle Paul states it helpfully in that we are to "bear one another's burdens, and in this way you will fulfill the law of Christ" (Gal 6:2).

"I don't want to be a burden" is an often-repeated dread in our individualistic society in which personal autonomy is emphasized above mutuality within community. One of the "hidden" aspects of discipleship exposed by dementia is our mutual dependency, our need of one another. To be human is to be a burden!

Psychiatrist/theologian Warren Kinghorn challenges the myth of personal autonomy with an alternative view of human interdependency and need for community:

> The remarkable thing about human life is not that humans are frequently a burden to each other, but that bearing each other's burdens is simply what humans do. It is care and relationship, not isolation and individualism, which are normative in human life. So, while it is true that caring for people with dementia (or supporting the caregivers of people with dementia) can be burdensome, it is also true that in these seasons the person needing care becomes more, not less, paradigmatically human.[9]

Christian discipleship involves bearing one another's burdens and permitting others to help bear our burdens. That's the dance of love! It also means the community worships, believes, and serves for the disabled disciple whose physical or intellectual impairments prevent him or her from participating in such visible expressions of discipleship. When persons with dementia can no longer recite the Apostles' Creed, the congregation recites it for them. When they cannot read the printed prayer, the congregation prays it for them. When serving on committees or mission projects exceeds their abilities, others serve on their behalf.

Dementia as Vocation

Sharing in the life and mission of the triune God is humanity's shared vocation. In the Christian tradition, we are baptized into Christ and, thereby, share in Christ's ongoing ministry through the power of the Holy Spirit within Christian community. We are recipients and mediators of God's salvation and participants in the triune God's holy dance of love, compassion, and justice.

Sharing in God's life and mission is contextual and communal. That is, our calling is within our own unique circumstances and takes place within a particular community. Each member of the community plays a significant role. The Apostle Paul's description of the community as a "body" with each part serving an important, indispensable function is appropriate (1 Cor 12). An often-ignored implication of Paul's image is the indispensability of the "weaker" or "less respectable members." As the apostle declares, "But God has so arranged the body, giving the greater honor to the inferior member" (1 Cor 12:24b).

Paul's declaration was written to a community located in the Greco-Roman world that highly valued intellectual acumen, rhetorical eloquence, and physical vitality. His declaration that God has chosen the "weak," "foolish," and "despised" as mediators of God's power, wisdom, and reconciliation was and is counter to the prevailing culture. It is precisely the weakest and least prominent whom God calls as disciples.

In speaking about the vocation of people with disabilities, Jean Vanier writes, "In some mysterious way, they [people with disabilities] are calling to me, to us all, to change.... When we meet people with disabilities and reveal to them through our eyes and ears and words that they are precious, they are changed. But we too are changed. We are led to God."[10] In this mysterious dance of the triune God's life and mission, those with dementia and other "disabilities" play an indispensable part.

Do people affected by dementia have a divine calling, a vocation? Certainly, caregiving is a sacred vocation! Linda's diagnosis represented a calling for me to evaluate how I would now best fulfill my baptismal and ordination vows. Her growing dependency and loss of cognitive functioning was my new context for ministry. My discipleship would now include learning about diseases that caused dementia, being attentive to and supportive of Linda whose discipleship had included support and attentiveness to my ministry, and sharing my own learning and experience with others. It meant relinquishing a cherished faculty position, narrowing the circle of institutional involvements and relationships, and relocating near our supportive family.

Caregiving is the archetype of Christian discipleship. It is the vocation of all who seek to follow Jesus, who defined discipleship as servanthood (Matt 20:24-28). The model is Jesus washing the feet of the disciples and calling the disciples into a life of humble service (John 13:1-20). Caregivers of the severely disabled are the epitome of self-emptying service, entering the most vulnerable areas of a person's life and performing the most intimate and unglamorous of services.

In entering that world of total vulnerability, a special bond of unique intimacy often develops. While caring for Linda includes times of frustration as she resists the invasion of her privacy, some of my most profound moments of connection come while brushing her teeth, grooming her hair, or feeding her her favorite ice cream. In that dynamic of giving and receiving, the bond between us grows and I sense a transcendent presence. Linda's acceptance of my aid and her occasional smile or whispered "thank you" are expressions of her discipleship.

Professional caregivers have become my heroes! Many of them consider their work as a calling, and those persons are easily distinguished from those to whom caregiving is only a job. Caregivers are in short supply, and this represents a major crisis in our aging society. Their role is underappreciated and inadequately compensated. To recognize caregiving as a sacred vocation and caregivers as indispensable participants in the triune God's dance of love can contribute immeasurably to the quality of life of those with disabilities as well as those who give aid.[11]

Persons in the severe stages of dementia fulfill their discipleship primarily in simply being! As they receive the care of others, they are participating nonetheless in the dynamic dance of love. Their receiving of care expands the caregivers' capacity to love without reciprocity, enables growth in patience and kindness, calls forth gentleness and attentiveness, and facilitates the presence of God in "the least of these."

Persons in early- and mid-stage dementia share actively in many forms of ministry. During one of my visits with Linda in the assisted living facility, I found her in the room of another resident. John and Linda shared the same diagnosis, frontotemporal dementia; and his behavior frequently created problems for other residents and staff. He and Linda, however, seemed to intuitively identify with each other. On this occasion, John wasn't feeling well and was lying in his bed. Linda was standing over him, gently stroking his arm. I paused at the doorway and listened as she said,

"I want you to feel better. I love you!" One who received care was providing care!

Another resident was a retired nurse. She routinely made "her rounds" each evening as people were readying for bed. She helped "tuck them in," and each morning she returned to make their beds. She helped fold clothes, clean tables after a meal, and always sensed when someone wasn't feeling well. Her embedded practices as a nurse continued and contributed to the well-being of the community.

A man in his nineties and a veteran of World War II was especially attentive to Linda during her time in the memory care facility. His days were spent walking around the unit and out into the courtyard. He was soft-spoken, gentle, and always very calm. He seemed to sense Linda's anxiety and fear and tendency to withdraw from social interaction. So, he came often to her room and asked her to walk with him. He repeatedly told the staff, "If she needs me, you let me know." His calm and parental presence provided a needed ministry to Linda, and to me.

My friend Dale continues his vocational calling as an ordained pastor and mental health chaplain. Both his father and his brother died after many years of living with Alzheimer's. Dale knew that he was at risk for the disease, and in 2010, the diagnosis confirmed his suspicions. Though saddened by the diagnosis, he made a conscious decision to "make the most of it." With the full support and encouragement of his wife, Norma, a social worker with training and experience in gerontology, Dale chose to be open and transparent about his disease. He entered a medical trial at Emory University, thereby contributing to research.

As part of the preparation for the progression of the disease, Dale and Norma moved into a retirement community where continuous care would be available. They participated in the multiple activities with their neighbors. While in the early stage, Dale served as a lector in the Sunday worship services. His sense of humor, sociability, and personal warmth endeared him to the community, and his presence contributed greatly to the quality of the community. He participated in the leadership of the seminary class on pastoral care and dementia and provided a unique perspective to the students.

As Dale's disease has progressed, the number of his activities has decreased as have his cognitive and language skills. He now lives entirely in the present moment and understands few words. Nevertheless, his social skills remain evident as he meets and greets people with warm smiles and friendly banter. He sings familiar hymns and other music with enthusiasm. He participates in the weekly worship services at Bethany where his wife accompanies hymns on the flute. He greets residents with a cheerful smile and "God is with you." He assists in serving Communion as he holds the cup as I dip the wafer for each participant. He continues his baptismal and ordained vocation! His way of being is an expression of Christian discipleship.

These are but a few indications that calling and vocation remain amid dementia. As with discipleship, dementia reveals "hidden" aspects of calling and vocation. The call is *to be*, and it is through our being that we fulfill our calling as disciples and share in Christ's ministry, even when our context includes Alzheimer's and other forms of dementia.

Conclusion

Dementia has changed the way Linda and I live our discipleship and vocations, but it has not diminished our participation in the triune God's dance of love. In many ways, our participation in God's love and mission has become more holistic as we have been challenged beyond the idolatry of abstract creedal formulations, excessive individualism, and perceived autonomy. We have come to an experiential discipleship and vocation motivated and formed by love lived in community and expressed in simple acts of compassion, caring, and presence.

My primary vocation is that of providing care for Linda. The care consists of meeting basic needs with kindness, gentleness, and sensitivity to her dignity. Providing for her comfort and safety and advocating on her behalf occupy my constant attention. Being present with her, assuring her that she is valued and loved, is at the heart of my daily activity. Other times, it is simply sitting quietly beside her and holding her hand while she sleeps. It also involves caring for myself by eating properly, exercising, arranging respite, and accepting support of others.

My discipleship and vocation spill over into relationships with others who live with dementia and sharing with them in the triune God's dance of love. The love Linda and I share with each other generates an expanding solidarity with others in similar contexts; and I am learning anew that in God's economy no act of love is ever wasted.

Linda's discipleship and vocation now are simply *to be* and to receive the love of others. Although some tasks may become burdensome, Linda is never a burden. She is a means of grace, God's presence and power to create, reconcile, forgive, and transform others who choose to be present with her. Her presence with us in her dependency is teaching us what it means to be a person made in the divine image and loved by God, and she is enabling us to grow more fully in love for God and neighbor. She is wooing us to love one another as Christ loves us.

Chapter 9

Dementia and the Church: Where People with Dementia Belong

Introduction

The church has been integral to Linda's life. She was baptized as an infant, confirmed as a youth, married in the church as an adult. She attended church camps, participated in church youth groups, and graduated from a church-related college with a degree in Christian education. She has taught Sunday school, trained teachers of children, served on committees, participated in outreach ministries, and faithfully fulfilled her membership vows. Indeed, her life's story cannot be told apart from her relationship with the church. However, dementia has robbed her of active participation in the community that has played the central role in her life. Does she really belong anymore?

Every congregation has members like Linda, and the numbers are increasing as the population ages. The median age of adult participants in mainline denominations is approximately fifty-six, which is ten years older than the median age of the adult population in the United States. The percentage of members who are over sixty-five is around one-third.[1] According to the Alzheimer's Association, one of every ten adults age sixty-five and older has Alzheimer's or another form of dementia; and one-third of older adults die with a form of dementia.[2] A typical mainline congregation with a membership of two hundred will include seventy who are sixty-five or older. Of that number, seven will have Alzheimer's disease. Add the members of the family who are significantly impacted by those seven people and the effect on the congregation grows. Those members are often relegated to the margins of the congregation's life and mission, and their gifts and needs are rarely acknowledged.

Yet, the church is strategically positioned to make a significant difference, and people affected by dementia potentially play a vital role in the life and mission of the church. When they really belong, the church is transformed, and their lives are enriched. Becoming a dementia-friendly church where people with cognitive impairments and their families belong is a theological and ecclesial opportunity and challenge. Confronting the challenges and opportunities requires revisiting the nature and mission of the church and developing intentional strategies for incorporating people impacted by dementia in the life and activities of local congregations.

The Church: A Called Community Where the Vulnerable Belong

The church is a community rooted and grounded in God's mission of reconciling, healing, and transforming the whole creation. The Bible chronicles God's calling and empowering vulnerable and marginalized people as recipients and agents of God's salvation.

It was in their old age that God called Abraham and Sarah to leave their homeland and to be the progenitors of a new community that would be a light to all nations (Gen 12). God called a fugitive murderer working as a shepherd, Moses, to be an agent of liberation of a community of slaves. Those slaves were led out of bondage and formed into a nation as an instrument of God's revelation and mighty acts of salvation.

When the nation was taken into exile, a remnant of the faithful became means of reconciliation and restoration. It was not through the nation's military or economic or intellectual might that God manifested the divine nature and mission. Rather, it was through Israel's frailty, woundedness, and weakness that God's nature and mission were made known.

The significance of the vulnerable, frail, and weak in God's unfolding salvation is clearly revealed in Jesus. He was born among the homeless of a peasant teenage mother and grew up in a remote village among working people. As an itinerate rabbi, he called a diverse and obscure group of twelve flawed disciples. He was executed as a criminal and buried in a borrowed tomb. Even in his resurrection, he was mistaken as a gravedigger or gardener.

The church exists as the community called to embody the presence of the risen Christ and through the Holy Spirit to continue the work of Christ in the world. The uniqueness of the Christian community lies in its call to be "the body of Christ" (1 Cor 12:27), a visible sign and instrument of God's presence and mission. As the "body of Christ," the church bears the marks of vulnerability, frailty, woundedness, and suffering.

The Apostle Paul states clearly that the presence of the vulnerable, weak, and "foolish" as members of Christ's new community is essential. To a congregation located in the Greco-Roman culture that valued intellectual acumen and individual capacities, he wrote the following:

> But God chose what is foolish in the world to shame the wise, God chose what is weak in the world to shame the strong. God chose what is low and despised in the world, things that are not, to reduce to nothing things that are, so that no one might boast in the presence of God. He is the source of your life in Christ Jesus, who became for us wisdom from God, and righteousness and sanctification and redemption. (1 Cor 1:27-30)

In the same letter, Paul declares that the weakest and most vulnerable members of Christ's body are indispensable: "The members of the body that seem to be weaker are indispensable" (1 Cor 12:22). Not only are the weakest and most vulnerable to be included as members of the body, but also they are to be given greater honor and treated with the utmost respect (1 Cor 12:23-24). Rather than being relegated to the margins, God in Christ has made them the center of Christ's new community.

People with dementia are among the most vulnerable, invisible, and forgotten in our congregations. Yet, they are among the very people who belong at the center of the community's life and mission if the church is to be the body of Christ. When they truly belong, they become our teachers and vital participants in the divine mission.

Jean Vanier, who devoted his adult life to being present with people with disabilities, contends that "the weakest and least presentable people are indispensable to the church,"[3] and they have something crucially important to say to our society. Vanier adds, "In some mysterious way, they are calling to me, to us all, to change."[4]

People with disabilities are our teachers and means of healing and liberation, if we are willing to be present with them and receive their gifts. But what contribution can possibly be made by people whose capacities for active participation are severely limited by diseases? What gifts do they bring to the life and mission of the church?

Gifts of People with Dementia

The supreme gift anyone brings to the life of a community is his or her being. That runs counter to conventional utilitarian thought that treats everything, including persons, as commodities to be valued for their usefulness in the world of production. Worth and value depend on contributions to the bottom-line financial or programmatic goals. In church, faithfulness is often measured by the contributions made to the institution's metrics—attendance, financial contributions, participation in activities. To contribute means to sing in the choir, attend or teach classes, serve on committees, participate in public events, share in mission projects, and so on. Presence means adding to the metrics.

In God's economy, value and worth lie in grace, a gift! Rather than everything being measured by utilitarian value in the marketplace of commodities, all of creation is valued as a gift to be celebrated, nurtured, and shared for the common good. What if we approached every aspect of God's creation as containing inherent mystery, meaning, and beauty from which we can learn and grow? That would mean each person, regardless of capacities, would be viewed as our teachers and avenues of God's gracious presence.

Should that not be how we view one another as members of the body of Christ? Each person is a unique gift whose very existence is a unique means of divine presence and a contribution to the common good. The very presence of people with dementia adds to the church's rich diversity, thereby expanding the imagination and broadening participation in God's life and mission.

The presence of people affected by dementia challenges many of the presumptions and practices of the church. As we have attempted to demonstrate, their presence pushes us to a deeper understanding of the essence of the Christian faith, challenges the idols of rationalism and doctrinal abstractions, strips us of the illusion of individual autonomy, and reminds us that human worth lies in bearing the image of God, not in physical and intellectual capacities. Their presence confronts us with our own frailty and interdependency. They teach us the value of the present moment and the enduring and healing power of love.

An additional contribution of those with dementia is their authenticity and genuineness. Alzheimer's and other forms of dementia strip away pretense and rationalizations and expose the impulses, feelings, and longings hidden deep within. Boundaries and filters vanish, and the realities of human frailty and limits are displayed. Intellectualism and rationalization used to avoid confronting stark realities of the human condition melt away, and habits of the heart dominate.

It is precisely the authenticity and genuineness of persons with dementia that contribute to their marginalization. Responses are unpredictable, and behaviors may be embarrassing. Carefully orchestrated order can be abruptly disrupted. Verbal communication is often garbled and unintelligible in the circumstances. While participation in some public events may be inappropriate, learning to accommodate the lack of inhibitions and the range of emotions expressed by people with dementia expands the congregation's empathy and hospitality.

First United Methodist Church in Montgomery, Alabama, initiated a respite ministry for people with dementia. It is staffed primarily with volunteers from the congregation. Participants include members of various denominations, the local synagogue, and avowed atheists. In commenting on the contributions of people with dementia to the life of the congregation, one of the pastors remarked, "Dementia doesn't discriminate but affects people with varied backgrounds equally. Because of that, it has caused church members to realize their common humanity with people who don't think alike or look alike, but who love and weep alike."[5] The congregation's sensitivity to and welcoming of "the other" has been enhanced by the participation of people with dementia.

One congregation I served as pastor included both pre-school and adult day care programs. The adult program consisted of people with dementia, and the facility was located near the playground used for the children's day care program, with a glass wall separating the two groups. Each day's schedule included the children leaving the playground and joining the adults. Joyful laughter and the exchange of gentle hugs filled the room. It was the highlight of the day for both the vibrant young and the frail old. The effects in terms of growth in understanding, empathy, and quality of life rippled through families, staff, and the entire congregation.

What are the gifts that people with dementia offer to the church? Their very presence exposes our idols of intellectualism and personal autonomy and reminds us that the essence of human identity and worth lies in God's grace. They challenge us to deeper understanding and experience of the basic tenets of the Christian faith. Their authenticity and genuineness strip away our own pretense and rigidity. They teach us the value of each moment and call forth our empathy, compassion, and patience. They break down the distinctions of age, class, race, and capacities, which routinely separate us, and help to form us into the body of Christ, a visible sign of God's reign of compassion, generosity, hospitality, and justice.

Nurturing a Dementia-Friendly Church[6]

Fostering a community in which the gifts of people with dementia are received and celebrated requires intentionality. Congregational life is usually characterized by order, decorum, prescribed practices, and abstract thinking. Worship and educational activities rely heavily on written communication and the ability to follow directions, whereas people in mid- and late-stage dementia lose vocabulary and ability to follow prescribed directions. People with dementia simply do not "fit in" without deliberate effort to foster a climate of acceptance.

An atmosphere of belonging for people with Alzheimer's and other forms of dementia emerges from clear theological understanding of the church as a community of Christ in which all belong. Christian community is God's gift through the Holy Spirit who in Christ has already made us one. Living the oneness wrought in Christ involves affirming the inherent worth and dignity of each person as a beloved child of God made in the divine image and encompasses the welcoming and honoring of his or her gifts. When that core message is proclaimed and embodied in practices, a climate of acceptance emerges.

Theological understanding must be supplemented with basic knowledge of dementia, if the congregation is to be welcoming of those affected by neurocognitive diseases. Congregations that celebrate diversity deliberately learn the culture of those who are different from the dominant culture. That is no less true of people with dementia. Entering the world of the cognitively impaired and their families and caregivers is like entering another culture with differences in language, worldview, habits, behavior, and needs. Education is necessary to remove the fear of the other and welcome their gifts.[7]

Remembering Those Who Are Forgetting

An initial step in fostering inclusion of those affected by dementia is identifying who they are. Because of the stigma attached to forms of dementia and the accompanying denial, people with symptoms are most often hidden from the congregation. They drop out of activities and withdraw from participation. Members and staffs of congregations lose contact with them or intentionally avoid them out of their own misunderstanding, discomfort, or inability to communicate with them. Soon, their presence is no longer missed. They join the ranks of the forgotten.

"They don't know that we exist," remarked a man whose wife is in mid-stage of Alzheimer's when asked if he hears from their church. The congregation of which they were once vital participants no longer remembers them. Forgetting those who are forgetting contradicts the message of a God who declares: "Do not fear, for I have redeemed you; I have called you by name, you are mine" (Isa 43:1).

The church is the steward of memories, especially memories of God's acts of salvation of individuals, communities, and the whole creation.

Included in the story of God's salvation is God's awareness of and concern for every person. As a visible sign and instrument of God's presence and mission, the church is to exemplify God's love for and attentiveness to the uniqueness of every person.

John Swinton writes, "The church... is the only community that exists solely to bear active witness to the living memory of Jesus. As such, it should be the place to see what God's memory looks like."[8] The church, then, is uniquely called to be attentive to those who forget and who are forgotten by society. Swinton adds, "The memory of God creates a community of remembering that is called to learn what it means to be attentive to God in those whose memory is no longer their defining feature or primary learning experience."[9]

The initial action in nurturing a dementia-friendly congregation is simply to know those within the community who are living with dementia. Remembering them as God remembers requires entering their worlds, learning their stories, and valuing them as mediators of God's grace-filled presence. Such remembering involves strategies, programs, and practices that equip the congregation to fully welcome and incorporate those with Alzheimer's and related diseases and their families.

Suggested Strategies and Practices

As congregations become informed regarding neurocognitive diseases and their impact and identify those living with the diseases, the needs to which the church can respond come to the forefront. Then begins the process of developing a vision and actions that respond to the emerging needs. The following are some ways churches are currently involved that have proven beneficial to those with the diseases and transformative to congregations.

Assess Congregation's Hospitality

Developing specific strategies requires an initial assessment of current needs and opportunities. Since people with dementia are invisible to most congregations, their gifts and needs go unnoticed. Therefore, an awareness of those affected by dementia within the congregation and community requires deliberate study of the local context. Who are they? What is their current level of participation? Where are they in the progression of the disease? What is their support system? How is the family affected? Are they in the home or a care facility?

The assessment also includes an evaluation of the church's availability and openness to people with dementia. Are the physical facilities readily accessible to people with impaired mobility and perception? Are public events, including worship and fellowship events, accommodating to people with cognitive challenges? What current activities and groups are inclusive of people with dementia?

The survey of local context also involves identifying groups, agencies, and institutions in the broader community that address people with dementia. The local Alzheimer's Association is an invaluable resource as is the state or local council on aging. What nursing homes and memory care facilities exist in the area? What ministries are being offered in those facilities? Are there ways the local congregation can complement those ministries? What are other local churches doing?

From the assessment will likely surface specific opportunities to which the congregation can respond. The assessment, however, should avoid the temptation to objectify the people with dementia by developing paternalistic responses. Any assessment must include consideration of the gifts and contributions of those living with dementia. Partnership, dialogue, and mutuality are the goal.

Support Groups

Caring for people with dementia is stressful, exhausting, and isolating. Studies over the last two decades of the effects of caregiving on family members have concluded that caregiving constitutes a national health problem in the United States.[10] The detrimental effects on the physical, mental, emotional, and relational health of caregivers are well-documented. The isolation and feeling of helplessness are pervasive.

Churches are well positioned to counter the deleterious consequences of caregiving by intentionally supporting family members. One such organized method of aiding is hosting a place for caregivers to gather and share their feelings. The local Alzheimer's Association is a willing and eager partner in such an effort, even providing trained group leaders and in some situations making funds available to provide a "sitter" while the family member attends.[11]

As one who has been part of support groups for more than six years, I can testify to the benefit. Gathering with people who share similar struggles and needs is an invaluable source of support and emotional health. Such participation diminishes the sense of isolation and offers assurance that "you aren't alone." While such groups are not considered "therapy," they do enable participants to vent feelings of frustration, anger, guilt, and helplessness in an atmosphere of confidentiality and mutual support.

Support groups for people who are in the early stages of dementia are also needed, and they are much less readily available. Most support groups include only family members and not the person diagnosed with the disease. The diagnosis is shocking and frightening for the individual diagnosed, and he or she needs special support. Dealing with the shock, denial, and anguish with others confronting similar challenges can be very helpful in overcoming the denial and feelings of hopelessness.

Adult Day Care

A growing number of churches are offering adult day care programs, which are designed to provide care and companionship for older adults who need assistance or supervision. Not all such centers are designated exclusively for people with dementia, but those with cognitive impairments are among the most frequent participants. The goals are to delay or prevent institutionalization by providing alterative care, to enhance self-esteem, and to encourage socialization. While some adult day care programs offer intensive health, therapeutic, and social services for participants, those sponsored by churches more accurately fit the description of "adult social day care."[12]

Local churches that provide day programs for persons in early- and mid-stage dementia communicate to the congregation and broader community that persons with dementia matter. There are many configurations of such programs. Some operate every day for several hours each day with a full cadre of paid staff. Others are more limited in times of operation and rely mostly on volunteers. Congregations that intentionally integrate the weekday adult care program with the total life of the congregation are the ones that maximize the influence of the people with dementia on the church.

Respite Care

Family members of people with dementia need respite from the persistent demands of caregiving. Adult day care programs provide respite for family members, even though the focus is on the persons with dementia. First United Methodist Church in Montgomery, Alabama, offers a creative combination of adult day and respite, with caregivers receiving special attention. A uniquely creative aspect of the program is that people in early-stage dementia serve as volunteers in relating to people in a more advanced stage. Efforts are made to diminish the distinction between those with dementia and the caregivers and other volunteers. Barriers are overcome, and a community of mutuality emerges.[13]

A participant in the respite ministry at First United Methodist Church shared in an email a testimonial to the value of the ministry. The story is told by the husband:

> Respite has provided Bobbie and me an opportunity to become active in the church once again. As her dementia progressed, she began to lose so much weight that her clothes didn't fit and, because she was already small, we had difficulty finding clothes she could wear to church. I had been a part-time teacher in our small Sunday school class so we lost that social outlet when we stopped going to church on Sunday. We didn't stop attending entirely because she had always enjoyed the Wednesday night chapel service so that became our only contact with the church as a couple. I was a volunteer worker in the "Fix-it-shop" ministry, which happened to be on the same floor as the Respite Ministry. When it became obvious Bobbie was in decline, I made an effort while working in the shop, to find out more about respite by talking with the volunteers down the hall. It became immediately obvious that respite was exactly what she needed. As her health continued to decline, her friends became fewer, which I now know is typical of people

with dementia. Having been a very social person all her life, she was in desperate need of a social outlet opportunity. Respite fit the bill perfectly! She immediately joined as a "volunteer" and, as time passed, over the last year has become more and more a participant.... So, respite has been an answer to prayer by providing Bobbie an opportunity to serve and be served in ways too many to enumerate. When she had to stop driving soon after joining respite, life at home would have been a little like living in a prison for us both. Every morning, when I get her up from bed, she asks "am I going to respite today?" Happily, most mornings (the four days a week respite meets) I say yes. That makes her day and mine too. God provides...abundantly![14]

Simple Acts of Support

Adult day care and respite care ministries represent important responses, and they involve significant investment of institutional resources. Less intensive but no less significant means of welcoming people affected by dementia exist in every congregation. The following are a few ordinary expressions of inclusion that counter isolation, lend support, and maximize belonging:

1. Recruit, train, and support a cadre of visitors/friends of those with dementia and their families and maintain regular (weekly) contact with those confined to home or a facility.

2. Provide a weekly meal for families who care for loved ones with dementia.

3. Volunteer to sit with a person with the disease while the caregiver gets a break.

4. Sit with the person with dementia in worship and assist as needed.

5. Intentionally greet and welcome with a smile and genuine compassion those with dementia.

6. Simply treat the persons with dementia with kindness and enter their world with the expectation you will meet God among "the least of these."

Conclusion

One of the last words to leave Linda's vocabulary was *church*. Often the word surfaced among incoherent babbling, and it was impossible to know what triggered her to use the term. I suspect that deep within her being, church remains. Its message and practices have shaped her into who she is and continue to sustain her. Familiar hymns and other music play softly throughout the day. Each week a couple from the congregation brings a meal. When they enter her room, I say, "Linda, John and Emma are here from church. They brought us food. Emma used to sit with you in Sunday school and hold your hand." Emma gently strokes Linda's hair and tells her that she misses her, compliments her, assures her that she is loved. Until recently, the word *church* was included in Linda's jumbled verbal expressions for a couple of hours after the visit from John and Emma.

The same congregation sends us a handwritten note and photo regularly. Linda's name appears in large letters on the front of the crafted notecard. On an occasion several months ago when I showed her the card and commented, "It's from the church," she squinted her eyes as she looked. Then with pathos in her voice she said slowly, "Linda! That's me!" It was the last time she has read a word! In that fleeting moment, the church reminded her who she is and that she belongs!

Chapter 10

Dementia as Spiritual Challenge and Opportunity

Introduction

Linda and I have lived with dementia for more than a decade, almost a quarter of our life together. The journey entails many medical, social, physical, psychological, emotional, and financial challenges; and those challenges significantly impact every aspect of our lives. But, Alzheimer's and other forms of dementia cannot be reduced to a medical, financial, or social problem. The journey with dementia is a weighty spiritual journey with experiences of profound joy, deepened and expanded love, and heightened attentiveness to the presence of God.

Jane Marie Thibault and Richard L. Morgan[1] raise important questions, especially for the church: How can we deliberately make a paradigm shift from thinking of care for persons with dementia as a medical and social problem to viewing care as a spiritual opportunity, a challenge, an invitation for both caregiver and care receiver? How can we trust that caregiving is not an unwelcome glitch in a well-planned life? How can it be a way of living that is a mutual path of spiritual deepening, of coming closer to God, and of witnessing the love of God to each other and to the world? How can the person suffering from dementia participate? Such a shift has occurred in my own perspective over the last decade. What was once seen as an abysmal calamity, a dreadful intrusion into our serene world, I now view as a treacherous segment of a lifelong spiritual journey. Warren Kinghorn's image of "wayfarer on the way to God"[2] has helped to put the medical, financial, and social challenges in a broader frame. Those challenges remain. However, when seen through the wider theological, spiritual lens, they become potential pathways into God's presence and growth in relationship with God and others.

What about Linda's spiritual needs? While much attention is given to providing medical and other physical care for people with dementia, very little is done to nourish their spirits. The self-initiated practices that once provided inspiration, assurance, and hope recede with the advancement of Alzheimer's and other dementia illnesses. Prayer, personal devotions, reading of Scripture, and corporate worship fall by the wayside. How are people who forget God enabled to grow in relationship with God? What nourishes their spirits as these "wayfarers" continue their journey to God? It's an old question, raised by the psalmist, "Are your wonders known in the darkness, or your saving help in the land of forgetfulness?" (Ps 88:12).

Spiritual Needs in the Land of Forgetfulness

Many Christian denominations baptize infants, and other faith traditions have rituals of incorporating children into the covenant community. In those rituals, the congregation promises to surround the children with love and care and to nurture them in the faith. It is not a promise with a termination date; it is for life! Just as the promise is made without the child's awareness or understanding, the responsibility of the faith family continues when members can no longer remember who they are in relationship with God.

Congregations have ongoing programs by which people are formed and nourished in faith. Those programmatic efforts to fulfill the promise made in baptism are sensitive to the developmental stages of the participants. Multiple curricula and other resources are designed for children, youth, and adults. Yet, few programmatic activities and resources exist for those who live in the land of forgetfulness, those for whom diseases are inexorably erasing their memories and ability to think abstractly. Too often, they are cut off from the community in which their fundamental identity lies, and little is done to assist these wayfarers during the most vulnerable and treacherous segment of their journey toward God.

much like climbing a mtn.

During a seminar with pastors, I asked, "In what ways do you and your congregation meet the spiritual needs of members who live with dementia?" There followed a long period of silence. Finally, a pastor said, "We include them on our 'homebound' list and pray for them." When I asked if they or anyone from the church visits them, five of the approximately fifty pastors answered affirmatively. One participant remarked, "I really don't feel that it's a productive use of my time. I go occasionally to support the family, but I don't feel that I can contribute anything to the person with dementia."

During my four years as volunteer chaplain in a memory care facility, I have known of only a half dozen visits from pastors of the residents. During Advent and Christmas, a few local congregations bring choirs into the facility to "sing for the residents." Occasionally, a local church and pastor will provide a worship service "for the residents." During those occasions, there is little interaction with the residents and minimal effort to involve them in doing more than observing.

There seems to be a widespread assumption that people with dementia, especially those in the advanced stage, are void of spiritual needs, longings, or wishes. Yet, if human beings bear the divine image into whom God has breathed God's own Spirit, we are "ensouled bodies, embodied souls."[3] Failure to acknowledge and respond to the spiritual needs of people with dementia is to accept the Cartesian, mechanistic, and dualistic definition of personhood and limit their care to the physical body.

The leader of a seminar for caregivers stated, "The primary needs of your loved one with dementia are twofold—safety and comfort. The other needs have faded into the background. Just keep them physically safe and comfortable." During a question-answer time, I stated, "While I want Linda to be safe and comfortable, I also want her dignity to be preserved, and I want her to experience love and value and to have meaning and purpose. Can you suggest ways those basic spiritual needs can be met as her disease progresses?" The long silence indicated that the expert on dementia and caregiving had not entertained such a question.

What are the spiritual needs of people with dementia? Simply stated, they are the same needs we all share! The need to give and receive love remains throughout the journey. We are conceived and born from love; in love, we live and move and have our being, and love sustains us through death. "Love never ends" (1 Cor 13:8) and "Neither life, nor death, nor angels, nor rulers, nor things present, nor things to come, nor powers, nor height, nor depth, nor anything else in all creation, will be able to separate us from the love of God in Christ Jesus our Lord" (Rom 8:38-39).

Dignity remains a lifelong need of human beings. The stigma attached to dementia in our hypercognitive and capacity-valuing society robs people of their dignity. Holding onto that dignity is a formidable challenge as the diseases progress and dependency increases. What is often interpreted as resistance and difficult behavior is an attempt to preserve dignity. Toileting can be an especially sensitive matter, requiring exceptional skill and patience by caregivers.

As a beloved child of God bearing the divine image, every person regardless of physical or mental capacities longs for worth and dignity. Affirming dignity of others involves being present with them, calling them by name, valuing their uniqueness, receiving their gifts, assuring them that they are loved by God.

Our Scriptures provide limitless resources for nurturing the dignity of those with dementia. Recently, for the devotions at Bethany, I read Hebrews 13:1-2, "Let mutual love continue. Do not neglect to show hospitality to strangers, for by doing that some have entertained angels without knowing it." We talked about "angels" they have known in their lives. As I greeted each person individually, I called their names and said, "You are an angel to me." Their faces suddenly lit up and a sparkle came to their eyes.

A sense of meaning and having purpose are universal needs to which theology speaks powerfully. A survivor of the Nazi concentration camp at Auschwitz, Viktor Frankl, spoke at Wesley Theological Seminary when I was a student. He had just written the book *Man's Search for Meaning*. As a psychiatrist, he developed a system of therapy called logotherapy, which postulates that humans have an inherent drive or will for meaning. In an interview, he quoted from the philosopher Nietzsche, "He who has a *why* to live for can bear almost any *how*."[4]

When my friend and neighbor, Dale Sessions, was diagnosed with Alzheimer's, he made a conscious decision to "make the most" of his disease. He often stated, "It is what it is. I don't like it, but I've got it; so, I'll do the best I can with it." His vocation as an ordained clergy, his astute theological perspective, and his experiences as a mental health chaplain conditioned him to approach Alzheimer's as a theological and vocational challenge. He enrolled in a clinical trial program at Emory University as a means of helping to find a cure or treatment for others; and as we have seen in a previous chapter, he continues to have a pastoral presence among others with dementia. It gives him meaning and purpose.[5]

The Respite Ministry at First United Methodist Church in Montgomery, Alabama, relies heavily on volunteers. Many of those volunteers have been diagnosed with a form of dementia but are still able to function as contributors with other volunteers. The director comments that it is often impossible to tell who has been diagnosed from those whose disease has advanced. They become one community in fulfilling purpose and meaning.

But what about those in the advanced stage? What possible sense of purpose can they experience in their incapacitation and dependency? In the severe and advanced stage, one may not be able to direct the will toward a sense of purpose. How can Linda's need for a sense of purpose and meaning be met when she is unconscious of such a need?

My observation is that the drive for meaning is deeply embedded and transcends cognitive decisions. As we are creatures bearing the image of God and empowered by God's Spirit, our purpose lies in relationship with God. Fundamentally, our purpose is *to be* more than to do. Affirming that another's being has inherent meaning and brings joy, love, and purpose is a profound means of grace. I constantly assure Linda with expressions of affection, smiles, and laughter, that she brings me much joy and that I am happy to be with her. She may not always respond intellectually or with visible expression, but frequently she smiles, laughs, or squeezes my hand.

The embedded practices in which people find meaning continue beyond cognitive awareness or conscious choice. During early and mid-stages, those practices are evident. For example, Dale's lifelong desire "to

It's in the little things.

help others" manifests itself in his continuing social interactions. A retired nurse who now resides at Bethany and is in mid-stage is attentive to another resident's distress. A former music teacher of children brings cheer as she walks the hallway humming familiar tunes.

Responding to the need for purpose and meaning requires knowing the stories of those who have forgotten their past. Furthermore, it requires finding ways to connect to and facilitate the practices that have provided them meaning.[6] That requires moving beyond focus on their losses and deficiencies and identifying and acknowledging their gifts, accepting them as contributors to the community, whether in an institutional setting or among the family.

The need to belong is universal and transcends cognitive capacities. As we have stated previously, individual autonomy is a myth. We are born within families, live within communities, and are inevitably connected to one another. We are social creatures, and belonging is a lifelong need. Yet, the stigma associated with dementia isolates people and cuts them off from sustaining relationships. Nurturing a sense of belonging among people is a challenge, for the symptoms often include behaviors that are embarrassing for the person with dementia and those who relate to them.

In the early stages of Linda's disease, she was aware of the difficulties in communicating and the weakened filters that resulted in questionable or inappropriate comments. I was sometimes embarrassed by her comments and behaviors. Gradually, we withdrew from social engagements. On one occasion, she blurted out amid sobs, "I don't belong anywhere anymore! I just want to die!" I hugged her as we both cried, and I wondered if either of us really belonged anymore.

How do we reassure those who live with dementia that they really belong when society seems to say that only the cognitively capable have a place? The church verbally proclaims a message of belonging rooted in the inherent worth and dignity of all human beings, regardless of capacities; however, people with dementia become invisible in most congregations, compounding a sense of rejection and worthlessness. Congregations must, therefore, develop intentional, programmatic practices that assure people with dementia that they belong.

Spiritual Needs of Caregivers

According to a 2015 study, 43.5 million adults in the United States provided unpaid caregiving to an adult or child in the prior twelve months.[7] Twenty-six percent report caring for someone with Alzheimer's disease or other form of dementia or memory loss.[8] The emotional, physical, financial, and spiritual strain on caregivers is incalculable. Failure to adequately deal with the strain can result in diminished health of the caregiver.

The adverse effects of caregiving have been well-documented. Studies by the Family Caregiver Alliance, National Center on Caregiving, report higher levels of depression and increased risk of chronic diseases such as heart disease, diabetes, and cancer among those who provide unpaid care for a family member.[9] Among the feelings reported by caregivers are the following: guilt, loss of self-esteem, diminished sense of purpose, constant worry about future, uncertainty, lost confidence, inadequacy, grief, and hostility.[10]

It was the impact on my physical and overall well-being that prompted our daughters to insist that I get outside assistance for Linda's care. There were observable signs of deteriorating health such as loss of appetite and weight, sleeplessness, lower resistance to viruses, increased irritability, and growing detachment. I was becoming impatient with Linda, short-tempered, and frustrated. I occasionally spoke angrily to her and then felt terribly guilty for my loss of patience and emotional control. I was exhausted.

Admitting her to the memory care facility was accompanied by over-whelming feelings of guilt, loneliness, and grief. I left from my regular daily visits in tears, yearning for her peace and mine, anxious about her safety and well-being, grieving the loss of her presence. God seemed absent, unresponsive, irrelevant! I felt alone, even though family and friends surrounded me. Those were the lowest months of the long journey, my "dark nights of the soul."

It is difficult for me to imagine traveling this journey without a theological/spiritual perspective and the resources such a perspective provides. A strong grounding in the grace and unconditional love of God enables us to accept our own feelings and struggles and deal with the guilt accompanying the losses. One friend expressed it well, "Whatever you feel is real and it's okay to express it. Dementia sucks!" A clergy colleague who cared for his wife for ten years was especially helpful when he said, "Ken, if you ever need someone to go with you out behind the barn and just cuss, I'm available."

Both friends reminded me of the value of laments. The Psalms became daily companions, especially the laments! Journaling my feelings, including the anguished ones, became a form of prayer. Weeping, mostly alone and in private, cleansed the soul and relieved stress. Tears turn to prayers, as Job lamented: "My face is red with weeping, and deep darkness is on my eyelids; though there is no violence in my hands, and my prayer is pure" (16:16-17).

Although the temptation to withdraw is always present and spiritual practices often seem meaningless, I intentionally stay engaged. Every person's response and needs are unique, but we all need times of withdrawal and quiet as well as times of engagement and activity. Finding the appropriate rhythm for each person is important, but maintaining spiritual practices provides means of stability amid the surrounding chaos.

Indeed, caregiving intensifies spiritual needs and longings, but it also affords unique opportunities to grow in the "fruit of the Spirit…love, joy, peace, patience, kindness, generosity, faithfulness, gentleness, and self-control" (Gal 5:22-23). While I would not glamorize the struggles or diminish the heartache involved in caring for a person with dementia, neither would I negate the enormous spiritual gifts such a journey entails.

The essence of personal salvation is the restoration of the divine image, growth in Christlikeness and the fruit of the Spirit. Such growth is an endless process within circumstances filled with ambiguities, uncertainties, challenges, holding on and letting go, give and take, laughter and tears, life and death. The circumstances themselves have within them means of grace, the presence and power of God to create, reconcile, and transform.

When approached through a theological/spiritual lens and with a theological foundation, caregiving with dementia requires the exercise of such virtues as love without reciprocity, merciful humility, persistent patience, inexorable kindness, radical generosity, untiring faithfulness, extraordinary gentleness, and constant self-control. I, therefore, have come to see caregiving as a distinct and profound means of grace.

Worship in the Land of Forgetfulness: *With*, Not *For*

Human beings have an inherent need to worship, to connect with and celebrate something beyond themselves. I first heard the definition of *worship* by the late Archbishop of Canterbury, William Temple, when I was in seminary in the 1960s. Amid the destruction of the Second World War, the leader of the Church of England declared that worship was the world's greatest need. Such a declaration seems naively unrealistic until we ponder his definition of worship:

> To worship is to quicken the conscience by the holiness of God, to feed the mind with the truth of God, to purge the imagination by the beauty of God, to open the heart to the love of God, and to devote the will to the purpose of God.[11]

The definition expands *worship* beyond an activity confined to a specific time and place to an orientation toward life and reality, a way of being that connects to transcendent goodness, truth, beauty, and love. People with dementia need such connections and can respond to the rhythm and melodies of music, the color and fragrance of fresh flowers, the brilliance of a sunrise or sunset, the soft fur of a family pet, the aroma of freshly baking bread, and the presence of a small child. Such connections are forms of worship!

Those in the early and mid-stage can participate fully in corporate services of worship that are sensitive to their needs and capabilities. Such services require leadership that is flexible and open to spontaneity. Music is central as familiar music lingers long beyond the loss of other functions. Knowing the faith traditions of those who are present is important, for familiar liturgical practices are often embedded, including the posture of reverence, verbal responses, and creeds.

The weekly worship services at Bethany follow a familiar pattern as outlined below:[12]

Call to Worship: "This is the day the Lord has made, let us rejoice and be glad in it!" (We speak it verbally and then sing it to the familiar tune.)

Invitation for God's Presence: Sing "Kum Bah Yah"

Prayer of Invocation

Chorus: "Surely the Presence of the Lord Is in This Place"

Hymn of Praise

Prayers of Thanksgiving "What is something you are thankful for?" We all respond with "Thank you, God."

Doxology

Testimony of Faith (usually a familiar Bible verse stated in unison or Apostles' Creed or Psalm 23)

Hymn

Scripture Reading

Homily/Reflection (interactive and limited to about ten minutes)

Prayers of Intercession

The Lord's Prayer

Hymn

Benediction

Communion is served monthly and at special occasions. Following each service, I greet each worshipper personally, calling their names and offering a blessing. Often family members of residents share in the worship experience with their loved ones and members of the staff frequently participate. A housekeeper frequently sings a solo during the service and residents contribute in special ways, such as helping to arrange the altar or assist one another in arriving and leaving.

Local congregations play a significant role in providing worship opportunities for those with dementia. Designing services that are dementia-friendly involves less dependency on long written responses, and the use of familiar hymns, openness to spontaneity and improvisation, and authenticity on the part of the leadership. I am familiar with one congregation that offers a worship experience especially for people with dementia during the regular schedule of other worship services. This provides a respite for family members as well as an enriching worship experience for the person with dementia.

Conclusion

"Wayfarers on the way to God" encounter unexpected challenges, daunting obstacles, and deceptive detours. However, what often appears as an obstacle or detour becomes a pathway to deepened relationships and surprising growth. While the intrusion of dementia into our anticipated life together remains a source of grief and struggle for Linda and me, the journey has been and continues to be filled with life-transforming gifts. This segment of the journey has been an intense time of growth in my own understanding of myself, what it means to be a person, and the difference a theological lens makes in living joyfully and with purpose. The journey fosters growth in "the fruit of the Spirit"—love, joy, peace, patience, kindness, generosity, faithfulness, gentleness, and self-control.

The church is uniquely positioned to nurture the spiritual lives of those with dementia and those who care for them. With disproportionate numbers of members affected by dementia and its very nature as a community called to embody God's presence and mission, faith communities can provide what medicine alone cannot. But it isn't simply what the church can provide for those living with dementia; it is the gifts those persons bring to such communities. They are special bearers of God's grace!

Chapter 11
Dementia, Grieving, and Death

Introduction

"I'm losing her a brain cell at a time," I remarked to a friend early in the progression of Linda's disease. Slowly, relentlessly, all her mental and physical capacities have declined. It is as though a brilliant, multicolored light is gradually fading into an encroaching darkness. The process includes short periods of stability with only subtle changes, allowing time for adjustment to the losses. Then, inexplicably the rate of decline accelerates, and the dramatic losses surface more grief. The radiant light grows dimmer and dimmer, with occasional fleeting flickers of brightness. The reality of perpetual loss is unavoidable. Grief is, as Kenneth Doka declares, "the constant yet hidden companion of Alzheimer's disease and related dementias."[1]

I have been acutely aware of my own grief as spouse and caregiver. Our daughters and their families often speak of "missing" Linda, and their sadness is sometimes visible. We can talk with one another about the losses, regrets, and longing for "Linda as she used to be." But Linda's grieving is less identifiable as her ability to perceive and articulate thoughts and feelings disintegrates as the disease progresses. Signs of grief and sadness emerge, sometimes openly, other times subtly. I often see sorrow in her eyes, or she will occasionally whimper in grieving tones. Is she aware of her losses since only the present moment seems real? Do the tears flow from mourning, or is there another explanation?

Grief is no stranger to any of us. As pastors, we accompany people through the stages of the grief process, and as family members and friends, we experience the process personally. A growing corpus of literature on the dynamics of grief provides helpful insight and guidance. Yet, little is directly and specifically applicable to the pervasive and relentless grieving involved in living with dementia. Rituals exist to facilitate the grieving when a loved one dies; yet no rituals exist for the grief accompanying dementia.

How are we to understand the grief of persons with dementia? How does the grief vary from stage to stage? How can we aid in the process? What about the grief of family members and caregivers? What are sources of hope and comfort from the Christian faith? It is to these questions that we now turn.

Grief of the Person with Dementia

During the early stages of Linda's disease, elements of the grief process were expressly visible: shock, denial, anger, and guilt. A dramatic explosion of grief occurred when she failed the examination for renewal of her driver's license. The loss of driving privileges confronted both of us with the grim reality. It meant the loss of independence, freedom, and control. Initially, Linda faulted the Department of Motor Vehicles for being discriminatory toward the elderly. She even took the test a second time with the same result. She resisted the idea that her driving was a threat to herself and others.

The expressions of grief were often subtler as the losses multiplied—frustration at being unable to dress herself, tears when she realized she couldn't call a grandchild's name, anger at perceived shunning by friends, exasperation at the inability to find words or comprehend my words, defensiveness when I offered to help with a task she could no longer complete. Each lost capacity was accompanied by grief.

As the disease advanced, Linda's ability to comprehend and reflect on the losses faded, as did her capability to express her feelings verbally. It was as though her grief went underground and erupted in behaviors and expressions unrelated to specific incidents or losses. She became combative and hostile for no apparent reason, lashing out at me. It was as though life itself was against her, stripping away everything she valued; and she struggled between letting go and holding on.

Restlessness, withdrawal, searching, crying, waning appetite, and a forlorn look in her eyes were among the outward signs of underlying grief. "I want to go home" became a frequent plea, when we were at home. Over time I learned that "home" was more a feeling, an emotion, than a place. It was a longing for life as it once was, a sense of security, connectedness, belonging, comfort. Recently, Linda has verbally expressed, "I'm going to die" or "I want to die." While such expressions touched my own anticipatory grieving, I have tried to give her permission to let go and assure her that we will be okay.

Attentiveness to the feelings beneath the behaviors is the appropriate response to the grief of the person with dementia. Reassuring presence is the most helpful counter to their grief. Entering the person's world with empathy and compassion, gently mourning with him or her, a tender touch and warm embrace—these are means of countering the relentless grieving. The great tragedy is that the difficult behaviors emerging from the grief often drive people away, precisely at the time their presence is most needed.

The Grieving Caregiver

From the first indicators of Linda's cognitive impairment, grief has been my continuous companion. Sometimes the companion has kept a manageable distance; other times, it has been like a violent intruder. Often it is like a cumulus cloud floating silently and unobtrusively above me; other times, a reminder of a past shared experience triggers a thunderbolt of grief, leaving me sobbing uncontrollably. The lament of the psalmist has surfaced throughout the journey: "My tears have been my food day and night" (Ps 42:3a).

Pauline Boss, researcher and professor emeritus at the University of Minnesota, coined a term that aptly describes the grief loved ones of people with dementia experience: *ambiguous loss*.[2] She defines ambiguous loss as "a loss that is unclear; it has no resolution, no closure."[3] The person with dementia is both present and absent, gone but still there, beside you but far away. As Boss writes, "With dementia, absence and presence coexist....When someone you love has dementia, the task is to increase your tolerance for the stress of ambiguity."[4]

Ambiguous loss makes caregiver grief particularly confusing and lonely. It is a roller coaster of conflicting emotions, a continuous process of holding on and letting go, yearning for an end to the anguish while resisting the final goodbye. Spouses feel the ambiguous grief most poignantly, for the adjustments to ever-changing roles, behaviors, and responses make closure impossible. An accommodation to one change quickly requires another adjustment, and another, and another!

The ambiguous loss accompanying dementia contributes to a form of grief Kenneth Doka identifies as disenfranchised grief, which "refers to losses that are not appreciated by others." Doka writes: "The individual has no perceived 'right' to mourn; the loss is not openly acknowledged or socially sanctioned and publicly shared. Others simply do not understand why this loss is mourned and may fail to validate and support the grief."[5]

Society fails to acknowledge that the "long goodbye" is a legitimate grief process, thereby denying those on the journey support and means of grieving. I have often thought: "Why am I grieving? Linda is still with me. I should rejoice that I still have her." Yes, she is still physically present with occasional moments of emotional connection. Those moments of emotional connection are filled with ambivalence. They are profoundly joyful, while at the same time, their temporariness triggers deep sadness in anticipation of the final loss.

Caregiver grief is layered and multifaceted. Caregivers are grieving for the losses experienced by the one with dementia while also mourning their own personal losses. The loss of a primary conversation partner, lover, confidante, and life partner changes the caregiver's self-perception and role. Linda has been part of my identity for almost six decades, but that aspect of my own identity is altering as she changes. I've seen myself as her husband, but the role now is more that of a parent. I grieve for what is happening to her and what is happening to me! And, I lament that our daughters have lost much of their relationship with their mother; and our grandchildren no longer receive the generous expressed love of their grandmother.

Anticipation of the journey's end adds another layer to caregiver grief. "What's next?" is the lingering question. Some changes are stark reminders of the final loss. Linda frequently moves into a deep sleep, and I quickly check her pulse and listen for the next breath, wondering, "Is this the end?" "Will I be ready when the end comes?" is a constant query. Although we as a family have made plans for her death, the emotional response remains unpredictable.

The nature of the past relationship affects the grieving. Spouses of people with dementia grieve differently than their children. While our daughters love their mother, visit her almost daily, and mourn the changes taking place, their primary engagements are with their own children and professions. Their existence is less entangled with that of their parents and, yet, they continue to love and support them.

Linda and I, however, have lived in an intertwined world of mutual affection, interdependency, and shared history for six decades. As a neighbor whose wife has dementia said, "We've been joined at the hip for seventy years, and it feels like a slow amputation!" As Kenneth Doka writes, "Spouses may become 'crypto widows'—married in name but not in fact. They may grieve the losses associated with that role—losses of intimacy, companionship, and sexuality."[6]

Dementia changes the nature of the relationship, and new patterns of relating must be developed. One who was independent and self-reliant becomes dependent and insecure. Personalities may change, and one who was cooperative and congenial may become resistant and combative. Spousal grieving is a continuous process of letting go of the person who was and learning to love the person who is, while at the same time anticipating the final separation of death.

The patterns of relationships within families influence the grieving process. Families characterized by open communication and mutual support will naturally face the losses and attending grief with solidarity. Where there is a history of tension and alienation, the dementia will likely intensify the stress and complicate the grieving. Care of the loved one may disproportionately fall on one member of the family, potentially creating resentment, anger, and guilt.

Institutional placement adds another facet to the grieving process. My experience supports Doka's claim that the decision to place a loved one in a facility intensifies and complicates grieving.[7] When I could no longer provide the necessary care and safety in the home and my own health was deteriorating, admission to the facility designed to care for people with Alzheimer's and other dementias seemed to be the only alternative. The decision and process of admission were heart-wrenching, as were the eighteen months that followed.

Strong feelings of guilt emerged. I felt that I was failing her, abandoning her. The staff assured me that I could now concentrate on emotional support while they provided the everyday care. As the director said, "You have been her caregiver; now you can just be her husband." What she didn't seem to grasp was that I couldn't separate those; caring for her had become a way of being her husband, and now I was losing that part of the relationship and my identity.

Generally, institutions operate predominantly on a medical model, with controlling symptoms and meeting basic bodily needs as the focus. Staff members know little of the stories and peculiar characteristics of the residents; and they have minimal time to spend one-on-one with residents and families. Other residents are in various stages of their diseases, and such values as privacy and solitude are impossible to maintain.

It became clear that my role in the facility was advocacy on behalf of Linda and helping staff know her story. I wrote a letter to the staff describing who Linda has been and why she is important to me. Our daughter placed a poster on the wall above her bed entitled, "Talk to me about these." There followed a list of words or names that would most likely trigger a response from Linda: "Millie, my dog," "Emory and Henry College," "Crazy Patsy," "Sheri and Sandra, my daughters," and so on.

Linda's eighteen months in the facility involved a complicated grieving process. Guilt for placing her, anger at real and perceived neglect, frustration with systemic institutional problems, loneliness at her absence—these were among my feelings and struggles. It was largely disenfranchised grief, since few people seemed to understand the trauma involved in admitting a loved one to an institution. "You must feel relieved," commented a neighbor. On the contrary, I felt devastated!

Many people adjust and even thrive in the institutional setting. Linda declined. She didn't adjust to the communal living, and fear seemed to be a constant companion. Her unhappiness added to my grief and I left many visits in tears. While relieved I no longer had the physical responsibilities associated with her, I grieved her absence, her emotional distress and physical decline, as well as my own inability to adequately care for her.

Institutional placement often further isolates the person with dementia from family and friends. Pastoral visits are rare and once-faithful members of congregations are often forgotten, adding to the losses and accompanying grief. One family member said, "I feel like we've been excommunicated by our church." Family members are sometimes seen as intruders by staff members, or family may find the institutional setting "depressing" and stressful, with the result being fewer and fewer visits. As one family member commented, "I feel guilty for not visiting my dad more often, but I always leave depressed."

Grieving the Final Goodbye

The death of the person with dementia changes the focus of the grief. As with other phases of the journey, the grieving is individualized and multifaceted. Some people experience what one author calls "a liberating loss, characterized by feelings of relief and emancipation that caregiving responsibilities and suffering by both the patient and family have ended."[8] Others may grieve the loss of the caregiving role and experience a sense of meaninglessness and lack of purpose. A man who cared for his wife for almost a decade said when she died, "Now I feel totally lost. I don't know who I am anymore or what to do with myself."

Guilt is a common component of all grief, but it may be especially intense upon the death of a family member with dementia. Reminiscing about the long journey may surface times when more patience and empathy could have been shown or difficult behaviors tolerated. Regret for institutional placement or failing to provide more assistance or to visit more often contribute to the feelings of guilt. Even the feelings of relief may be accompanied by guilt for having such feelings.

The grief at the death of the loved one is sometimes disenfranchised or minimized by others who assume that the grieving has already taken place. Intended statements of support may complicate the process. Comments such as, "This must be a blessing," or "You must feel relieved," fail to acknowledge the complexity and depth of the survivor's grief.

Research has indicated that expressions of grief were different between those whose loved one died at home compared to those who were in a nursing home or memory facility. Those who were in the home reported "exhaustion, stress, anxiety, and anger"; while those in institutional care indicated higher levels of guilt and sadness.[9] Wherever the death occurs, it marks a turn in the grieving journey toward a future without the physical presence and regular interaction with the loved one. Memories of the past take on added significance since creation of new memories out of continued interaction has ceased.

Navigating the grief process inherent in Alzheimer's and other forms of dementia requires physical and emotional stamina, attentiveness of the multifaceted and layered nature of the grieving, and a resourceful community of support. The journey is a marathon requiring ongoing preparation and participation in the tasks of grieving.

Tasks of Grieving

While grieving is a complex emotional journey, it consists of identifiable tasks to be completed. Psychologist J. William Worden classifies four tasks of mourning. While the tasks he identifies refer to the grief resulting from the death of a loved one, they are relevant for the ongoing losses experienced in dementia. The tasks are as follows:

- Accept the reality of the loss.
- Work through the pain of grief.
- Adjust to an environment in which the loved one is missing.
- Find an enduring connection with the person while moving forward with a new life.[10]

Accepting the reality of the losses occurring throughout the journey with dementia is an ongoing challenge for both the person with dementia and those who care for them. The incremental and often subtle nature of the losses makes denial possible. However, as the disease progresses, the losses become more evident and disruptive. While rituals exist to mark the grief of the final loss, no such practices are available for confronting the gradual, more subtle losses.

A practice I have found helpful in accepting the reality and working through the pain is the use of lament. As Linda experiences a specific loss, I write a prayer in which I express my grief, sadness, even anger. Following the expression of lament, the prayer turns to thanksgiving for having been the beneficiary of the gift. For example, when she lost the ability to prepare meals, I bemoaned the absence of her delicious food and ability to prepare and serve it. Then the prayer became one of gratitude for having enjoyed her meals for fifty years and for her generous hospitality in sharing her culinary gifts with family and friends. Such a practice has helped me accept the reality of the losses as well as enabled me to move forward with thanksgiving.

There is no way around the pain of grieving; one simply must go through it! Grief is love mourning. Accepting grief as inevitable in a relationship of love doesn't remove the pain, but it does diminish its futility. Acknowledging the pain and expressing it within a supportive community enables those who mourn to move forward with comfort and courage. Lament and tears are therapeutic.

Keeping a journal of one's feelings is helpful for some as they work through the pain of grieving. Putting aching feelings into words, written and spoken, may clarify and assuage their intensity. Participation in support groups assists in coping with the pain, and it counters the sense of being alone. Pain shared is pain diminished.

The grief accompanying dementia requires persistent adjustment to an environment in which the person is different rather than "missing." As stated previously, the person you miss is still with you, but dementia is ever altering the behavior, abilities, and interactions. With each loss in capability comes a change in the relationship requiring accommodation.

While death signifies a closure, the losses from dementia are open-ended, and the adjustments to the new reality are ongoing.

A neighbor spends two to three hours each day visiting his wife in the memory care facility. His life revolves around those visits. Someone remarked to him, "You need to get on with your life," implying that he was failing to adjust to the reality of his wife's lost functioning. "This is my life," he retorted. "She's changed, but she's not dead," he added. It is evident that he lives in two worlds at the same time—a world including his wife and a world apart from her. Finding peace and meaning in both worlds is the challenge.

When death occurs, the bereaved remains connected with the deceased primarily through memories. One moves forward by integrating those memories with new experiences, relationships, and activities. The grieving task for those living with dementia is finding ways of connecting with the changed person as he or she is now, while letting go of former ways of connecting.

The enduring bond transcends cognitive and physical capacities. The connections of shared memories, activities, and relationships slowly recede as the disease takes its toll. The memories are now held by the loved one and thereby provide a connection, but the lasting bond transcends cognitive and physical capacities. Identifying and nurturing that transcendent bond is key to the grieving process.

Love: The Bond That Endures

The theological lens broadens the perspective and provides comfort and hope. At the core of the Christian tradition is the affirmation that love is the dominant and eternal reality in all creation; human beings are created to participate in the triune God's dance of love. The Epistle of First John declares, "God is love, and those who abide in love abide in God" (4:16b). The Apostle Paul declares that nothing "in all creation, will be able to separate us from the love of God in Christ Jesus our Lord" (Rom 8:39).

Theologian Norman Wirzba offers a helpful definition of love as understood in the Christian tradition:

Love is the power that enables us to affirm, even embrace, the wide range of life's splendor and tragedy. It is the passion that enables us to protect, nurture, and celebrate every created thing. It is the lens that enables us to see each person and creature as a gift worthy to be cherished. Love is the eternal "yes" to life's possibilities and promise.[11]

According to Weny

Love is the paradoxical reality throughout grief's journey. Love creates the pain of grief, and love motivates care and support amid the pain. Love mourns the cascading losses while embracing the inherent worth of being itself. Love laments the shattering of the world as it has been while opening pathways into the world as it is becoming. Love struggles to hold close the one who is drifting away, and love yearns for his or her ultimate peace. Love bewails the powerlessness to prevent the inevitable, and love dares to trust that "weeping may linger for the night, but joy comes with the morning" (Ps 30:5b).

Hope lies in the final triumph of love over all that threatens God's intention for creation. Christian hope derives from God's presence within human experience and God's victory over sin and death in the life, death, and resurrection of Jesus the Christ. It is "the assurance that God does not abandon the world but is committed to healing its wounds."[12] Confident trust that the wounds will finally be healed and that death does not have the last word provides comfort and courage amid persistent and final loss.

Intimations of the final triumph of love abound for those who remain vigilant and attentive to signs of emotional connection as memories fade, glimmers of coherence amid confusion, flickers of joy within the surrounding gloom, traces of harmony amidst dissonance. In loving the vulnerable other, we are participating in the greater love in whom we live and move and have our being. In such moments, the eternal enters the transitory and fills it with enduring promise and a peace that passes comprehension.

Conclusion

"I feel like I'm living a perpetual funeral," sighed the spouse whose husband of sixty years is in the late stage of Alzheimer's disease. She added, "Every day brings another loss and a reminder of the end that awaits." Her comment rings agonizingly true for all those who live with Alzheimer's and other forms of dementia.

Since the first signs of dementia, Linda and I have been accompanied by "the hidden and constant companion" of grief. Linda's consciousness of the grief companion seems to have faded as the disease has gradually lessened her cognitive awareness. Paradoxically, among her losses may be awareness of the pain of grieving those losses.

I and our family, however, continue the relentless, ambiguous, multi-faceted, and many-layered process of grieving. Sometimes the grief hovers in the distance like a thin cloud only faintly dimming the brightness of the sun. Then comes another loss or an intimation of the journey's end. The grief descends like a funnel cloud, blocking the sunlight and whirling us uncontrollably into a painful new reality.

Acknowledging the losses and addressing the tasks of grieving require attentiveness to one's own feelings, avenues for expressing the feelings, and supportive community in which the feelings are understood and accepted. Viewing grief as integral to love and a participation in the transcendent love of the triune God means that the grieving process can be a means of growth in love. Furthermore, the conviction that God is persistently working for healing and wholeness and will bring to completion the new creation begun in Jesus Christ fosters hope.

"You are providing a womb of love for Linda as she is being birthed into another world," suggested Karl Netting, a friend and longtime hospice chaplain. The image helpfully describes the overarching goal of the grieving process. People living with dementia are gradually and inexorably moving toward another world, a mysterious new reality for the person with the disease and those who care for them. Expanding the lens to include birth of the new while letting go of what has been adds purpose, hope, and comfort to the grieving process.

Chapter 12

Dementia and Reframing Pastoral Care and Theology

Introduction

People with Alzheimer's and other dementia diseases existed on the remote margins of my thirty-five-year ministry as a local church pastor. There was less public awareness during the last half of the twentieth century when I served as pastor; and my engagement with dementia was limited to a few parishioners' families and my elderly grandmother who had "hardening of the arteries." Admittedly, I felt insecure visiting people with dementia, and I assumed that my absence made no difference to them or their families.

The last two congregations I served as pastor, however, were ahead of me. They both developed day programs for people with dementia. While I was supportive, I saw the participants as recipients of "mission," and they were ancillary to the ongoing activities of the congregation. The directors were far more visionary and knowledgeable than I.

After a decade's journey with the forgetting and forgotten, I am convinced that they are among those who live at the center of God's presence, memory, and mission. They are integral, therefore, to the church's nature and mission; and pastors play a key role in ministry with this growing population and in shaping congregations where such people truly belong.

What follows is a return to and expansion of some themes addressed in previous chapters, especially chapter 3. The suggestions are directed primarily to pastors and church leaders, and they are based on my personal experience of being present with the forgetting and forgotten over the last decade. I am convinced that through our presence with them we are transformed by the God who has chosen the weak and powerless as special means of transforming grace.

Confront Our Own Fears of Dementia

The high priority our society places on individual capacities, personal autonomy, and productivity contributes to the widespread stigma and fear associated with dementia. Pastors and church leaders are not immune to the fear. The fear can motivate positive efforts to combat forms of dementia such as advocacy for research and treatment, practicing a healthy lifestyle, and countering the stigma and stereotypes of those with the diseases. But fear can also paralyze, foster denial, and lead to avoidance of people with dementia, thereby adding to the devastation and isolation accompanying the disease.

The first step in overcoming fear is acknowledging it. While I early recognized the subtle changes in Linda's capacities and behaviors, I was initially unable to acknowledge my fear. I thereby contributed to the denial and delay in making important decisions; and, I felt uncomfortable in the presence of others who exhibited similar symptoms as Linda. As I shared with a trusted friend my concern about Linda's health, he asked, "What are *you* feeling, Ken?" Immediately, I blurted out, "I'm scared. I think she has dementia." The question and response opened the floodgates of tears and launched an ongoing exploration of my fears for Linda and my own fear of dementia.

I suspect that the prevailing isolation and marginalization of people living with dementia are rooted in fear—one's own fear of personal cognitive decline and fear of not knowing how to relate to those with the disease. Acknowledging the fear opens the door to actions that counter it. Unacknowledged fear, however, contributes to the suffering and marginalization of people with dementia.

Seeing dementia through a theological lens enables us to face our fears with courage, assurance, and hope. Though the grief and pain remain throughout the journey, I can deal with my fear with the assurance that

assurance:
we are more than our capacities; we are not alone; love endures; and our stories are connected to the story of God's mighty acts of salvation.

Learn about Dementia

A lack of knowledge contributes to fear and failure to pastorally engage people with Alzheimer's and other forms of dementia. When Linda was diagnosed, I couldn't spell *Alzheimer's* and had never heard of frontotemporal dementia. She and I both shared the stigma associated with the term *dementia*. We knew little of what awaited us, and I had little understanding of how to best support her.

Pastoral care with people living with dementia requires basic knowledge of dementia. Few seminaries offer courses directly applicable and even Clinical Pastoral Education rarely includes exposure to people with dementia. Limited continuing education opportunities exist to fill the void. Therefore, pastors and others involved in pastoral care are left largely on their own initiative and resources.

Many sources of basic information exist and are easily accessible.[1] The most important source, however, are the people in our congregations. Every congregation has people to whom dementia is a lived reality, and they are our most important teachers. Learning from them requires presence with them.

Prioritize the Ministry of Presence

The most effective ministry among people living with cognitive impairment is presence. The power of presence is incalculable, both for persons with dementia and the ones present with them. The ministry of presence, however, is devalued in our utilitarian-oriented approach to relationships and ministry. Ministry is often viewed as solving a problem, motivating and facilitating change, and doing something for those in need. When viewed thusly, presence with the cognitively impaired will be disappointing and perhaps demoralizing.

Dr. Benjamin Mast, a clinical psychologist and associate professor in geriatric medicine at the University of Louisville, emphasizes the importance of being present with those who have Alzheimer's disease and their caregivers. He writes: "When I interview caregivers and ask what the church can do for them, the most common response is: They simply want the church to be present in their lives through the journey with dementia. They do not want to be alone."[2]

Pastoral presence is about *being with* rather than *doing for*. The goal is to receive others' gifts, experience God's grace present in and through them. Although he is writing about presence with homeless persons, Sam Wells's words are equally relevant for those with dementia:

> You don't sit and have a coffee with a homeless person because you're trying to solve their problem—you do so because you want to receive the wealth of wisdom, humanity, and grace that God has to give you through them. You aren't the source of their salvation: they are the source of yours.... Your every effort is to enjoy their being, and share your own, rather than change their reality assuming a script you've imposed from elsewhere.[3]

An exasperated pastor confessed her frustration with visiting people with dementia. "I feel so powerless! I can't do anything for them. I pray with them, but they often don't even know what I'm doing when I pray." Perhaps our powerlessness is the strength of our presence! To set aside our agendas, relinquish our preconceived expectations, and simply be with another in his or her world is the essence of incarnational ministry. Such powerless presence is the context in which divine grace has room to grow and transform. As the Apostle Paul declares, "My [God's] grace is sufficient for you, for [my God's] power is made perfect in weakness" (2 Cor 12:9).

Presence with people who have dementia takes time and energy. Entering their world requires intentionality and concentrated attentiveness. More than the presence of the ordained clergy is necessary. If I were a local church pastor, I would identify, recruit, train, and support a cadre of laity to specialize in being present with those living with dementia and their families. A team similar to Stephen Ministers would be the primary pastoral presence on behalf of the ordained and the congregation. I would publicly recognize the team and liturgically commission them for such ministry, thereby giving such ministry visibility and theological validation.

Shift the Margins with the Vulnerable at the Center

People on society's margins are frequently seen as objects of the church's mission. We admonish congregations to journey to the margins and be present with those deemed as outsiders—the poor, the imprisoned, the immigrants, the sick, the vulnerable and powerless, and those with dementia. They become objects or targets of programmatic emphases but remain on the periphery of the congregation's ongoing life.

What is needed, however, is to shift the margins so that those on society's periphery become the center of the church as community. Rather than being targets of a programmatic or missional emphasis, the outsiders become insiders and integral to the total life of the congregation. As John Swinton describes:

> He [Jesus] certainly sat with those whom religious society had excluded and rejected as unclean and unworthy of attention. However, in sitting with such people, Jesus, who was and is God, actually shifted the margins. By shifting the margins with the pushed-aside at the center, the religious authorities became the marginalized! They didn't realize that Jesus had moved the margins to a totally different place.[4]

Presence with those with dementia and their caregivers requires going to them, but it also means bringing them into the life of the congregation. If God has chosen the weak and vulnerable to transform the strong and the foolish and confused to convert the wise, then those deemed as "the least of these" belong front and center in everything the church is and does. A church that shifts the margins to fully include those with dementia will:

- be well-informed about dementia;
- design worship services responsive to the cognitively impaired;
- assess and receive the gifts of those with dementia;
- make all activities accessible to those with cognitive impairment;
- be present with those absent from congregational activities; and
- teach, preach, and embody God's preferential presence with "the least of these."

Form Pastoral Care Congregations

My understanding and practice of pastoral care was shaped in the 1960s and '70s when the psychotherapeutic model dominated. Trained in counseling and active listening skills, I saw myself as the primary deliverer of pastoral care whether visiting parishioners in their homes, at the hospitals and nursing homes, or in my office. My generation of pastors fostered the notion and expectation that pastoral presence was the special responsibility of the ordained clergy with laity on the receiving end of the care.

Such an individualized, professionalized approach to pastoral care, however, falls woefully short of the pastoral presence needed in any congregation. For one thing, no professional staff can possibly be meaningfully present in all the places where shepherding care is needed. Additionally, it fails to fully appreciate the communal dimension of pastoral care and inadvertently contributes to the marginalization of people whose incapacities prevent them from participating in corporate worship and fellowship. The goal, therefore, is the forming of caring communities of faith that provide pastoral care.

Calling forth and shaping such communities is at the heart of the ordained pastor's role. Pastors are set apart to enable congregations to fulfill their nature and mission as a sign, herald, foretaste, and instrument of God's salvation. Clergy, therefore, are ordained to develop and nurture communities of pastoral care. They are to "order" the life of the congregation as a caring community that loves as Christ loves.

The shaping of caring communities requires different skills and practices from the traditional psychotherapeutic model of pastoral care. Facilitating the motivations and skills of others within the congregation becomes the priority of the pastor. Much of the caring done by congregations takes place in existing groups—Sunday school classes, women's and men's groups, small study groups, and so on. Helping such groups to see themselves as deliverers of pastoral care and equipping them to do so are core responsibilities of the ordained clergy.

Advocate for the Powerless and Voiceless

Advocacy on behalf of the powerless and voiceless is a prophetic dimension of pastoral care. Pastors and congregations are uniquely positioned to counter the medicalizing, stigmatizing, dehumanizing, and commercializing of people with dementia. As we have seen, society views people with dementia primarily through a medical lens with the focus on symptoms and diminished capacities. Responses fall under the category of "medical care," and institutional care mimics the hospital.

While medicine plays an important role in the care of people with Alzheimer's and other diseases, theology offers a more wholistic approach. Advocating for the inherent worth, dignity, respect, and belonging of all persons regardless of their capacities pushes beyond marginalization and toward inclusion and belonging. The mere presence of pastors and congregations in the homes and institutions where people with dementia live changes the dynamics and testifies to the *imago Dei* present in all of God's beloved children.

Advocacy for favorable governmental policies and funding is a legitimate function of the church. The cost of care is beyond the resources of the average family. According to a 2017 survey, the following is the average cost of various long-term care options:[5]

$235 per day ($85,775 annually), semi-private room
$267 per day ($97,455 annually), for private room
$3,700 per month ($45,000 annually), in assisted care facility
$22 per hour for home health aid
$70 per day for adult day care

The financial burden placed on families adds to their stress, and society must respond to this growing public health crisis. Local congregations and church leaders have a role to play in educating and advocating for healthcare, taxation, and other policies that alleviate the financial load placed upon families.

Join and Form Networks of Advocacy and Support

Many organizations and foundations are in the forefront of research, advocacy, and treatment related to Alzheimer's and other forms of dementia. A growing number of denominations and faith communities are joining the efforts to expand understanding and care; and some medical schools show signs of acknowledging the spiritual dimensions of dementia. Many local, state, and national governments are involved, such as councils on aging, the National Institutes of Health, Center for Disease Control, and public health agencies. The Alzheimer's Disease Education and Referral (ADEAR) Center is a service of the federal government's National Institute on Aging (NIA), one of the National Institutes of Health. The Center provides accurate, up-to-date information about Alzheimer's disease and related disorders to patients and their families, caregivers, healthcare providers, and the public.

The Clergy Against Alzheimer's Network and Faith United Against Alzheimer's Coalition are diverse interfaith communities for faith leaders and organizations advocating for dementia-friendly congregations and calling for action to prevent Alzheimer's. The local and national Alzheimer's Association are eager to work with faith communities in providing educational programs and advocating on behalf of legislation and policy changes. These and many others are available for networking with congregations to provide information and resources.

Most local congregations have nursing homes and memory care facilities within their parish boundaries and have members who are residents and staffs of those facilities. Most facilities are eager to have volunteers who supplement the care provided by staff. Networking with the administrators and staffs can radically alter the vision, morale, and effectiveness of those institutions.

Effective networking is a means of living the theological affirmation that God's presence and work are not limited to the institutional church. The church is called to join God's work of justice and compassion in the world among various institutions and agencies. Joining with governmental and other agencies responding to people with Alzheimer's disease and other dementias has the potential to transform congregations and agencies as well as broaden the lens and expand the care provided those with dementia.

Re-imagine Theology

Engaging with dementia during the last decade has impacted every area of my life, including how I do theology. We all do theology from our personal, social, and cultural contexts. Reviewing more than fifty years of ministry, I realize how much the varying contexts have shaped my theological perspectives and pastoral practices. Living with and ministry among people with dementia has been and continues to be an intense theological journey; I share ways the experience is impacting how I understand and do theology.

First, theology is lived more than thought, a way of being more than a way of thinking. Intellectual beliefs, doctrinal formulations, abstract declarations, and reasoned reflections are important; however, they are not the heart and soul of theology. They represent attempts to conceptualize and verbalize realities that surpass the confines of human thought and language. Theology is about transcendent mystery, ultimate meaning, and infinite connections; and those realities exist when thinking, reasoning, and language cease. Pastoral theology observes and appreciates the mystery, meaning, and connections inherent in the concrete experiences of everyday life with its limitations and frailties. How does someone whose mind has been lost "have the mind that was in Christ Jesus"?

Second, lived theology is more implicit than explicit. That is, the theology by which people live and act may not be the same as the consciously held and verbally communicated beliefs and affirmations. Though the goal is congruence between the implicit and explicit theology, motivations and actions result from multiple factors beyond intellectually held concepts. Discovering and connecting with the realities that underlie motivations and actions is a central role of pastoral theology. Where is God present and active in persons' lived realities, including those who have forgotten God?

Third, theology is embedded in the body as well as in the mind. Theology consists of bodily activities as surely as cognitive reflections, touch as well as thoughts, emotions as surely as ideas, hidden longings and visible behaviors, unconscious responses and chosen commitments. People with dementia express their theology primarily through their bodies more than their intellectual or verbal coherence. Sensitivity to and nurturing of bodily expressed theology is a critical pastoral role. People with dementia teach and express a bodily theology for those willing to listen and learn.

4,

Fourth, in the Christian community, we do theology for and with people. Christian doctrines, beliefs, and practices belong to the faith community, not simply to individuals. Clergy are ordained to preserve, interpret, defend, and proclaim in word and deed the church's doctrines and practices. It is the community that wrestles with the foundational theological questions—Who is God? Where is God? What is God doing? What is the appropriate response to the nature, presence, and purposes of God? And, it is the community that lives the answers to the questions.

When individuals within the community are unable to consciously affirm the beliefs, doctrines, and practices, the community does it for them. For example, those in the advanced stages of dementia lack the capacity to cognitively understand and articulate the theological affirmations. The congregation, however, affirms and practices those affirmations on behalf of those unable to do so. Each Sunday as we gather to worship, the congregation worships on behalf of those unable to participate. While those with cognitive impairment lack the capacity to engage in theological reflection, the congregation engages for them.

Fifth, the core of Christian theology is the practice of love. Christian love is a lived reality, not an abstract intellectual concept. If God is love, then such actions as caring, respectfulness, attentiveness, faithfulness, justice, kindness, and mercy are theological practices. Pastors are doing theology when they are present with the weak and vulnerable as surely as when they are exegeting Scripture or interpreting the doctrine of the Trinity. Forming compassionate and hospitable congregations that love as Christ loves is a most profoundly faithful theological act.

This also means that persons with limited cognitive functioning are no less theologians than professional academic theologians. To enter the world of those with dementia with attentiveness, compassion, and respect is to meet God, who has chosen the weak and vulnerable, the pushed aside and stigmatized as special revelations and profound means of grace.

Conclusion

As we have affirmed, Alzheimer's and other forms of dementia are vast medical, economic, and societal challenges. There is growing awareness of "the Coming Alzheimer's Tsunami."[6] Physicians and other healthcare professionals are keenly aware of the challenges represented by dementia, and researchers are devoting resources to prepare for this "tsunami." Advocacy groups are emerging to help change public attitudes and policies directed toward people with dementia and those who care for them.

A group largely absent from the important discussions and engagements are local church pastors and congregational leaders. Yet, they are the ones strategically positioned to provide what is most lacking in the current perceptions of and relationships with people living with dementia. Pastors and congregations can broaden the lens through which dementia is viewed, provide caring communities that affirm the inherent worth and dignity of people apart from their mental and physical capacities, and advocate for societal policies and practices that enable the least and most vulnerable to flourish as beloved children of God.

Engagement with the cognitively impaired should not be seen as another responsibility to be added to already overloaded pastors and congregational leaders. Rather, it is an invitation to meet God in fresh ways, to experience the reality behind the church's doctrines, and to be transformed and renewed by love that endures when knowledge and language cease.

Chapter 13

Conclusion

As I write these concluding words, Linda sleeps calmly in the bed nearby. The familiar hymn tune "Finlandia" ("Be Still My Soul") plays in the background. It is an appropriate hymn as I reflect on the changes since that fateful day in November 2009 when we received Linda's diagnosis of frontotemporal dementia. The unwelcomed ten-year journey has included majestic mountain peaks of joy and deep valleys of heartbreak, times of calm serenity and periods of traumatic restlessness.

Dementia has impacted every aspect of our lives and continues to influence how we feel, relate, believe, and behave. Although Linda's ability to comprehend, communicate, and interact is now severely limited, her very being continues to inform, inspire, and enrich my life. We, as family and extended community, now hold her memories and foster her identity as a beloved child of God with inherent worth and dignity.

This turbulent decade has been one of learning at the deepest level of understanding and growth in the experience of love and commitment. While I will not gloss over the intense pain, I want to affirm that there is life after a dementia diagnosis! No disease can destroy the essence of that which gives life meaning—joy, hope, and love!

Theology provides the lens necessary for me to endure this treacherous journey with joy, hope, and love. Locating our story within the story of God's nature, action, mission, and presence gives meaning and sustenance for the journey. Viewing dementia through the theological lens enables me to affirm the following:

- Medical science is a God-given resource for understanding and addressing the complex causes, symptoms, and treatments of diseases resulting in dementia; but dementia is more than a disease of the brain,
and human identity cannot be reduced to medical evaluations.

- Mind and memory are more than physiological components of autonomous individuals.

- Dementia challenges many theological affirmations and deepens our understanding and experience of divine grace.

- The triune God continues to bring order from the chaos, bondage, and exile inherent in the experience of dementia.

- In the incarnation, God claims all life as the domain of the divine presence and purposes and provides the paradigm for our presence with one another.

- Human identity, dignity, and worth do not lie in cognition and capacities, but in the *imago Dei* and God's claim of us as beloved children.

- People with dementia are both recipients of God's salvation and contributors to our own wholeness and spiritual growth.

- People with dementia have a calling and vocation as Christian disciples, even if they forget God.

- The church is strategically positioned to provide a community of belonging where the gifts of the cognitively impaired are celebrated and received.

- Meeting the spiritual needs and receiving the gifts of those with dementia require intentional presence and ministry of pastors and congregations.

- Grief is the constant companion of those with dementia and their families, and the faith community offers resources for living courageously and hopefully amid the grief and loss.

The most sustaining and transforming affirmation is the Apostle Paul's declaration: "Love never ends" (1 Cor 13:8). Love transcends intellectual and physical capacities and endures even when knowledge, memories, and language fail. The first verse of a hymn written by Mary Louise (Mel) Bringle and set to the same "Finlandia" tune playing in the background as I sit beside Linda's bed is a fitting benediction:

> When memory fades and recognition falters,
> when eyes we love grow dim, and minds, confused,
> speak to our souls of love that never alters.[1]

Notes

Foreword

1. Kosuke Koyama, *Three Mile an Hour God: Biblical Reflections* (Maryknoll, NY: Orbis, 1979), 7.

2. Koyama, 6.

3. Koyama, 5.

4. Koyama, 5.

Introduction

1. Alzheimer's Association, *2019 Alzheimer's Disease Facts and Figures*, annual report. See www.alz.org/alzheimers-dementia/facts-figures.

2. *2019 Alzheimer's Disease Facts and Figures.*

Chapter 1

1. World Health Organization, "The ICD-10 Classification of Mental and Behavioural Disorders: Clinical Descriptions and Diagnostic Guidelines," 2019, 46, www.who.int/classification.icd/en/bluebook.

2. National Institutes of Health: National Institute on Aging, "What Is Dementia? Basics of Alzheimer's Disease and Dementia," https://www.nia.nih.gov/health/what-dementia. NIH is an authoritative source of the latest research and information about dementia and other health syndromes and diseases.

3. D. F. Swaab, *We Are Our Brains: A Neurobiography of the Brain, from the Womb to Alzheimer's* (New York: Spiegel and Grau, 2014), 3.

4. Swaab, *We Are Our Brains*, 3.

5. "Beautiful 3-D Brain Scans Show Every Synapse," YouTube video, National Geographic, January 30, 2014, https://www.youtube.com/watch?v=nvXuq9jRWKE&feature=youtu.be.

6. National Institutes of Health, National Institute on Aging, "Diagnosing Dementia," reviewed December 31, 2017, https://www.nia.nih.gov/health/diagnosing-dementia.

7. National Institutes of Health, National Institute on Aging, "Biomarkers for Dementia Detection and Research," reviewed April 1, 2018, https://www.nia.nih.gov/health/biomarkers-dementia-detection-and-research.

8. National Institutes of Health, National Institute on Aging, "How Is Alzheimer's Disease Treated?" reviewed April 1, 2018, https://www.nia.nih.gov/health/how-alzheimers-disease-treated.

9. National Institutes of Health, National Institute on Aging, "Assessing Risk for Alzheimer's Disease," reviewed May 19, 2017, https://www.nia.nih.gov/health/assessing-risk-alzheimers-disease.

10. National Institutes of Health, National Institute of Neurological Disorders and Stroke, National Institute on Aging, "The Dementias: Hope through Research."

11. For a brief visual portrayal of what happens in the brain as the result of Alzheimer's, see the following video produced by the National Institutes of Health: "How Alzheimer's Changes the Brain," YouTube video, National Institutes of Health, August 23, 2017, https://www.youtube.com/watch?time_continue=84&v=0GXv3mHs9AU.

12. Alzheimer's Association, *2019 Alzheimer's Disease Facts and Figures*, https://www.alz.org/alzheimers-dementia/facts-figures.

13. From William Blake's four-line poem, "Eternity," www.poets.org/poetsorg/poem/eternity.

14. *2019 Alzheimer's Disease Facts and Figures*, 43, fig. 10.

15. *2019 Alzheimer's Disease Facts and Figures*, 43.

16. *2019 Alzheimer's Disease Facts and Figures*, 44.

17. Cathleen M. Connell, Mary R. Janevic, and Mary P. Gallant, "The Costs of Caring: Impact of Dementia on Family Caregivers," *Journal of Geriatric Psychiatry and Neurology* 14 (Winter 2001): 179.

Chapter 2

1. Plato, *The Republic* (380 BCE), https://www.spaceandmotion.com /Philosophy-Plato-Philosopher.htm.

2. Merriam-Webster, s.v. "mind," last modified April 7, 2019, https:// www.merriam-webster.com/dictionary/mind.

3. Additional discussion of mind/body dualism will follow in chapter 6.

4. Howard Robinson, "Aristotelian Dualism," *Oxford Studies in Ancient Philosophy* 1 (1983): 123–44.

5. John Swinton, *Dementia: Living in the Memories of God* (Grand Rapids, MI: Eerdmans, 2012), 61, 62.

6. See Susan Grove Eastman, *Paul and the Person: Reframing Paul's Anthropology* (Grand Rapids, MI: Eerdmans, 2017).

7. Stephen E. Fowl, *Philippians* (Grand Rapids, MI: Eerdmans, 2005), 90.

8. *Mosby's Medical Dictionary*, 9th ed. (2009), s.v. "memory."

9. Swinton, *Dementia: Living in the Memories of God*, 208.

10. Swinton, *Dementia*, 202.

11. Quoted in Swinton, *Dementia*, 190.

12. Charles Fernyhough, *Pieces of Light: How the New Science of Memory Illuminates the Stories We Tell about Our Pasts* (New York: Harper Perennial, 2012), 5f.

13. I am deeply indebted to John Swinton's *Dementia: Living in the Memories of God*. Swinton provides a compelling and thorough exploration of a "theology of memory" and its relevance for understanding dementia.

14. Swinton, *Dementia*, 214.

15. Swinton, *Dementia*, 217.

Chapter 3

1. David Keck, *Forgetting Whose We Are: Alzheimer's Disease and the Love of God* (Nashville: Abingdon Press, 1996), 15.

2. Warren Kinghorn, "'I Am Still with You': Dementia and the Christian Wayfarer," *Journal of Religion, Spirituality & Aging*, 2015, 6.

3. Karl Barth, "The Strange New World within the Bible," chap. 2 in *The Word of God and the World of Man*, trans. Douglas Horton (New York: Harper & Row, 1957), 28–50.

4. I am indebted to Dr. Randy Maddox for identifying the purposes of Christian doctrine. The information is in an unpublished outline of a class session at Duke Divinity School.

5. Kinghorn, "'I Am Still with You'" 11.

6. Kinghorn, "'I Am Still with You'" 11.

7. John Swinton, "What the Body Remembers: Theological Reflections on Dementia," ABC Religion and Ethics, June 26, 2013, 2. Also online at www.abc.net.au/religion/what-the-body-remembers-theological-reflections-on-dementia/10099780.

8. See *The United Methodist Hymnal*, 13–14.

9. Stated in the conclusion of Stanley Hauerwas and Jean Vanier, *Living Gently in a Violent World: The Prophetic Witness of Weakness* (Downers Grove, IL: Intervarsity Press), 20.

10. "The Need of Strangers," Jean Vanier's response to Stanley Hauerwas in John Swinton, ed., *Critical Reflections on Stanley Hauerwas's Theology of Disability* (Binghamton, NY: The Haworth Pastoral Press, 2004), 29.

Chapter 4

1. The comparison/contrast between the Augustinian or Western and Irenaean (Eastern) perspectives appears in John Hick, *Evil and the God of Love* (New York: Harper & Row, 1966).

2. John Swinton, *Dementia: Living in the Memories of God* (Grand Rapids, MI: Eerdmans, 2012), 184.

3. The Virtual Dementia Tour is a sensitivity training designed to help caregivers, family members, and friends understand what it is like to live with Alzheimer's and other forms of dementia. The participants' senses are distorted to simulate the effects of the disease.

4. Mark Price, "74-Year-Old Guilty of Killing Wife to Prevent Life as 'Caged Animal' in Nursing Home," *Charlotte Observer*, July 2, 2018.

5. Richard Lovelace, "To Althea, from Prison." The poem is in the public domain.

6. The survey was conducted in England by Disabled Living Foundation and reported by Andrew Hough, "More People 'Fear Losing Independence in Old Age Than Death,' Survey Says," *The Telegraph*, February 8, 2010. Informal surveys reported in Alzheimer's Association sources indicate similar results.

7. Gregory Mobley, "Know, Knowledge," in *Eerdmans Dictionary of the Bible*, ed. David Noel Freedman (Grand Rapids: William B. Eerdmans Publishing Company, 2000), 777.

8. W. Schottroff, "to perceive, know," in *Theological Lexicon of the Old Testament*, ed. Ernest Jennie and Claus Westermann (Peabody, MA: Hendrickson Publisher, 1997), 2:514.

9. Frederick Buechner, *The Longing for Home: Recollections and Reflections* (New York: HarperCollins Publishers, 1996), 2–3. The relationship between the home remembered and the home anticipated is discussed throughout the book.

10. Walter Brueggemann has lectured and written extensively on the theme of exile, theology, and culture. Among his books on the subject

are *Hopeful Imagination: Prophetic Voices in Exile* (Philadelphia: Fortress, 1986); *A Commentary on Jeremiah: Exile and Homecoming* (Grand Rapids: Eerdmans, 1998); and *Cadences of Home: Preaching among Exiles* (Louisville: Westminster John Knox, 1997). An excellent scholarly treatment of the role of exile in the formulation and theology of the Old Testament is by Daniel Smith-Christopher, *A Biblical Theology of Exile* (Minneapolis: Augsburg, 2002).

11. This basic theological declaration is the central theme of John Swinton's book, *Dementia: Living in the Memories of God*, although he does not relate it specifically to exile theology.

12. This and other helpful points are made clearly in a lecture by Walter Brueggemann delivered at Trinity Church, Boston, and accessible at https://www.youtube.com/watch?v=yw3ZiyXp-mE.

Chapter 5

1. Christopher Stead, "Logos," in *Westminster Dictionary of Christian Theology*, ed. Alan Richardson and John Bowden (Philadelphia: Westminster, 1983), 339.

2. The phrase *dwelt among us* comes from the same root as the noun *tabernacle* or *tent*, the place where God spoke to Moses (Exod 33:9) and where God's glory was seen (Exod 40:34).

3. Gail R. O'Day, "John," *New Interpreter's Bible* (Nashville: Abingdon Press, 1995), 9:524.

4. O'Day, 9:526.

5. Samuel Wells, *Incarnational Ministry: Being with the Church* (Grand Rapids, MI: Eerdmans, 2017), 7, 11.

6. Samuel Wells, "The Power of Being *With*: Jesus' Model for Ministry," *The Christian Century*, June 18, 2015, https://www.christiancentury.org/article/2015-06/power-being?reload=1559392891373.

7. Wells, *Incarnational Ministry*, 12, 13.

8. Judith Graham, "A Lonely Future? U. S. May See Rise of 'Elder Orphans,'" *Washington Post*, October 16, 2018. The data is based on a report by Northwell Health in New York and originally published in their online newsletter, https://www.northwell.edu/about/news/aging-baby-boomers -childless-and-unmarried-risk-becoming-elder-orphans.

9. Study by Dr. Joyce Varner, professor at the University of South Alabama, reported in article "The 'Elder Orphan' of the Baby Boom generation," by Carina Storrs, CNN, May 18, 2015, https://www.cnn .com/2015/05/18/health/elder-orphans/index.html.

10. This is a frequent statement by John Swinton, which I first heard in a lecture he delivered at Duke Divinity School, October, 2015.

11. Wells, *Incarnational Ministry*, 89.

12. Wells, *Incarnational Ministry*, 186.

Chapter 6

1. The Mini Mental State Examination (MMSE) is a widely used instrument to measure cognitive function. It is not seen as a diagnostic tool but rather as a preliminary assessment. It consists of a series of questions and requires only about ten minutes. The score ranges from 0 to 30, and a score below 10 is considered severe.

2. Warren Kinghorn, "'I Am Still with You': Dementia and the Christian Wayfarer," *Journal of Religion, Spirituality & Aging* 28, no. 1-2 (2016): 98–117. Kinghorn acknowledges the complexity of the causes of suicide; however, some studies indicate that the rate is highest among those segments of the population that prioritize individualism and personal agency.

3. The criteria are identified in Anthony Quinton, *The Nature of Things* (London and Boston: Routledge, 1973). Cited in Jennifer Hammer, "Absolute Personhood in Those with Dementia," *George Washington University Journal of Health Sciences* 6, no. 2 (July 2012), https://blogs .commons.georgetown.edu/journal-of-health-sciences/issues-2/vol-6-no -2-july-2012/absolute-personhood-in-those-with-dementia/.

4. Robyn Warner, "Locke, Brock, Personhood and Its Consequences in Justice for the Severely Demented Elderly," *Macalester Journal of Philosophy* 7, no. 1 (2010): 12.

5. Hammer, "Absolute Personhood in Those with Dementia."

6. John Swinton, ed., *Critical Reflections on Stanley Hauerwas' Theology of Disability: Disabling Society, Enabling Theology* (London: Routledge Taylor & Francis Group, 2004), 113–19.

7. William Ernest Henley, "Invictus," Poetry Foundation, www.poetry foundation.org/poems/51642.

8. Thomas Kitwood, *Dementia Reconsidered: The Person Comes First* (Buckingham: Open University Press, 1997), 7.

9. Kari Lislerude Smebye and Marit Kirkevold, "The Influence of Relationships on Personhood in Dementia Care: A Qualitative, Hermeneutic Study," *BMC Nursing* 12 (2013): 29.

10. Smebye and Kirkevold, 2.

11. Martin Buber, *I and Thou* (Mansfield Centre, CT: Martino, 2010).

12. Warner, "Locke, Brock, Personhood," 93.

13. John Swinton, *Dementia: Living in the Memories of God* (Grand Rapids, MI: Eerdmans, 2012), 144.

14. Kinghorn, "I Am Still with You," 10.

15. Jaroslav Pelikan, ed., *Luther's Works, Volume 1*, Lectures on Genesis, Chapters 1–5 (St. Louis, MO: Concordia, 1958), 61.

16. Susan Grove Eastman, *Paul and the Person: Reframing Paul's Anthropology* (Grand Rapids, MI: Eerdmans, 2017), 178f.

17. Kinghorn, "I Am Still with You," 12.

18. Swinton, *Dementia: Living in the Memories of God*, 197.

19. Dietrich Bonhoeffer, *Letters and Papers from Prison,* enlarged ed. Eberhard Bethge (New York: Simon and Schuster, 1997), 347f.

Chapter 7

1. Gerald G. O'Collins, "Salvation," in *The Anchor Bible Dictionary*, ed. David Noel Freedman (New York: Doubleday, 1992), 5:907.

2. O'Collins, "Salvation," 910.

3. John Wesley, "Farther Appeal to Men of Reason and Religion," *Wesley's Works*, vol. 8, bicentennial ed. reprint of 1872 ed. (London: Baker, 1992), 47.

4. John Wesley, "Letter to Alexander Knox (26 October 1778)," in *The Letters of John Wesley, AM*, ed. John Telford (London: Epworth, 1933), 6:327.

5. O'Collins, "Salvation," 908.

6. Elsa Tamez makes this point very clearly in her book *The Amnesty of Grace: Justification by Faith from a Latin American Perspective* (Nashville: Abingdon Press, 1993).

7. See Warren Kinghorn, "'I Am Still with You': Dementia and the Christian Wayfarer," *Journal of Religion, Spirituality & Aging* 28, no. 1-2 (2016): 98–117.

8. Quoted by Hans S. Reinders, "Being with the Disabled: Jean Vanier's Theological Realism," in Brian Brock and John Swinton, eds., *Disability in Christian Tradition: A Reader* (Grand Rapids, MI: Eerdmans, 2012), 487.

9. John Swinton shared this story in a lecture I heard him deliver at Duke Divinity School.

10. See also John Swinton, *Becoming Friends of Time: Disability, Timefullness, and Gentle Discipleship* (Waco, TX: Baylor University Press, 2016), 58.

11. Jolene Brackey, *Creating Moments of Joy for the Person with Alzheimer's or Dementia*, 4th ed. (West Lafayette, IN: Purdue University Press, 2007).

Chapter 8

1. John Swinton, "Gentle Discipleship: Theological Reflections on Dementia," ABC Religion and Ethics, July 11, 2016, https://www.abc.net.au/religion/gentle-discipleship-theological-reflections-on-dementia/10096784.

2. Daniel Goleman, "New View of Mind Gives Unconscious an Expanded Role," *New York Times*, February 7, 1984.

3. Swinton, "Gentle Discipleship."

4. James A. K. Smith, *Desiring the Kingdom: Worship, Worldview, and Cultural Formation* (Grand Rapids, MI: Baker Academic, 2009). Cited in Swinton, "Gentle Discipleship," 5.

5. The story is recounted in various sources, with slight variations in wording.

6. Swinton, "Gentle Discipleship," 5.

7. Swinton, "Gentle Discipleship," 4.

8. This expression is taken from the title of an excellent book by Jane Marie Thibault and Richard L. Morgan, *No Act of Love Is Ever Wasted: The Spirituality of Caring for Persons with Dementia* (Nashville: Upper Room, 2009).

9. Warren Kinghorn, "'I Am Still with You': Dementia and the Christian Wayfarer," *Journal of Religion, Spirituality, and Aging* 28, no. 1-2 (2016): 11.

10. Stanley Hauerwas and Jean Vanier, *Living Gently in a Violent World* (Downers Grove, IL: Intervarsity, 2008), 64.

11. If I were a local church pastor, I would designate a time during the year to recognize and consecrate caregivers during a service of worship, much as churches recognize and affirm teachers and other leaders. In the service, I would connect caregiving as a means of living our baptism.

Chapter 9

1. Michael Lipka, "Which U.S. Religious Groups Are the Oldest and Youngest?" Pew Research Center, http://www.pewresearch.org/fact-tank/2016/07/11/which-u-s-religious-groups-are-oldest-and-youngest/.

2. Alzheimer's Association, *2019 Alzheimer's Disease Facts and Figures*, https://www.alz.org/alzheimers-dementia/facts-figures.

3. Stanley Hauerwas and Jean Vanier, *Living Gently in a Violent World* (Downers Grove, IL: Intervarsity, 2008), 74.

4. Hauerwas and Vanier, 74.

5. Reverend Gillian L. Walters, email message to author, October 24, 2018.

6. Some denominations offer resources for ministry with people with dementia. For example, Discipleship Ministries of The United Methodist Church offers a helpful resource that may be accessed at https://www.umcdiscipleship.org/resources/the-dementia-friendly-church.

7. The Alzheimer's Association is an excellent resource for education and a willing partner with faith communities. Additionally, many states have a council on aging that provides materials and even financial support for families dealing with dementia.

8. John Swinton, *Dementia: Living in the Memories of God* (Grand Rapids, MI: Eerdmans, 2012), 222f.

9. Swinton, *Dementia*, 223.

10. Richard Schulz and Paula R. Sherwood, "Physical and Mental Health Effects of Family Caregiving," *American Journal of Nursing* 108, no. 9 (September 2008): 23–27, https://www.ncbi.nlm.nih.gov/pmc/articles/PMC2791523/.

11. The Alzheimer's Association is a valuable resource for caregivers in providing information and connecting with local resources.

12. US Department of Health & Human Services, Eldercare Locator, contains valuable information about various forms of adult day care and

locations of approved centers in local communities. See https://eldercare
.acl.gov/Public/Index.aspx.

13. As the director of respite ministries at First United Methodist
Church, Montgomery, Alabama, Daphne Johnston is available to share
information and other assistance to churches interested in starting respite
ministry.

14. Shared by Daphne Johnston in an email to author, October 24,
2018.

Chapter 10

1. Jane Marie Thibault and Richard L. Morgan, *No Act of Love Is Ever
Wasted: The Spirituality of Caring for Persons with Dementia* (Nashville:
Upper Room, 2009), 62.

2. Warren Kinghorn, "'I Am Still with You': Dementia and the Christian Wayfarer," *Journal of Religion, Spirituality & Aging* 28, no. 1-2 (2016):
98–117.

3. Kinghorn, "'I Am Still with You,'" 9.

4. See "Frankl: He Who Has a WHY Can Bear Any HOW," September 15, 2009, https://andreaskluth.org/2009/09/15/frankl-he-who-has-a
-why-can-bear-any-how/.

5. I did an interview with Dale Sessions when he was in the early
stages of his disease. The interview can be accessed here: https://www
.bing.com/videos/search?q=YouTube+interview+with+Dale+Sessions&
view=detail&mid=C01CFE54897757A3E1DCC01CFE54897757A3E1
DC&FORM=VIRE.

6. A helpful resource for connecting with people's stories and embed-
ded practices, including people with dementia, is Gary Chapman, *The
Five Languages of Love: The Secret to Love That Lasts* (Chicago: Northfield
Publishing, 2015).

7. National Alliance for Caregiving, *Caregiving in the U. S. 2015–
Executive Summary*, June 2015, 9, http://www.caregiving.org/wp-con

tent/uploads/2015/05/2015_CaregivingintheUS_Executive-Summary
-June-4_WEB.pdf.

8. *Caregiving in the U.S. 2015*, 12.

9. Family Caregiver Alliance, National Center on Caregiving, "Caregiver Health," https://www.caregiver.org/caregiver-health.

10. "Caregiver Health."

11. The definition is from Archbishop William Temple as recorded in my personal notes.

12. This order of service along with a commentary is part of an article written with Norma Smith Sessions entitled "Worship *With* Not *For*," published in Lynda Everman and Don Wendorf, eds., *Dementia-Friendly Worship: A Multifaith Handbook for Chaplains, Clergy and Faith Communities* (London: Jessica Kingsley Publishers, 2019).

Chapter 11

1. Kenneth J. Doka and Amy S. Tucci, eds., *The Longest Loss: Alzheimer's Disease and Dementia* (Washington, DC: Hospice Foundation of America, 2015), 79.

2. Pauline Boss, *Loving Someone Who Has Dementia: How to Find Hope while Coping with Stress and Grief* (San Francisco: Jossey-Bass, 2011). Dr. Boss coined the term in the 1970s, and she and others have expanded the research and deepened the insights. For more books that summarize the research and application, see Pauline Boss, *Ambiguous Loss: Learning to Live with Unresolved Grief* (Cambridge, MA: Harvard University Press, 1999) and Pauline Boss, *Loss, Trauma, and Resilience: Therapeutic Work with Ambiguous Loss* (New York: Norton, 2006).

3. Boss, *Loving Someone Who Has Dementia*, 1.

4. Boss, *Loving Someone Who Has Dementia*, 7.

5. Doka and Tucci, *The Longest Loss*, 85.

6. Kenneth J. Doka, *Living with Grief: Alzheimer's Disease* (Washington, DC: Hospice Foundation of America, 2004), 142.

7. Doka and Tucci, *The Longest Loss*, 83.

8. Doka and Tucci, *The Longest Loss*, 84.

9. Studies referenced in Doka and Tucci, *The Longest Loss*, 85.

10. J. William Worden, *Grief Counseling and Grief Therapy: A Handbook for Mental Health Practitioners, Fourth Edition* (New York: Springer, 2008), 39f.

11. Norman Wirzba, *Way of Love: Recovering the Heart of Christianity* (New York: Harper Collins, 2016), 7.

12. Wirzba, *Way of Love*, 201.

Chapter 12

1. Among the resources are the following: Alzheimer's Association, Clergy Against Alzheimer's Network (https://www.usagainstalzheimers.org/networks/faith); and National Institute of Health; and Council on Aging in various locations.

2. Benjamin T. Mast, *Second Forgetting: Remembering the Power of the Gospel during Alzheimer's Disease* (Grand Rapids, MI: Zondervan, 2014), 111.

3. Sam Wells, "The Power of Being With: Jesus' Model for Ministry," *The Christian Century*, June 19, 2015.

4. John W. Swinton, "Doing Small Things with Extraordinary Love: Congregational Care of People Experiencing Mental Health Problems," ABC Religion and Ethics, October 6, 2014, https://www.abc.net.au/religion/doing-small-things-with-extraordinary-love-congregational-care-o/10098938.

5. Alzheimer's Association, "Planning for Care Costs," https://alz.org/help-support/caregiving/financial-legal-planning/planning-for-care-costs.

6. Max Wallack, "The Coming Alzheimer's Tsunami," Alzheimer's Reading Room, April 10, 2013, https://www.alzheimersreadingroom .com/2013/04/the-coming-alzheimers-tsunami.html.

Chapter 13

1. Hymn lyrics are by Dr. Mary Louise (Mel) Bringle, who teaches philosophy and religious studies at Brevard College in North Carolina. See Donte Ford and C. Michael Hawn, "History of Hymns: When Memory Fades," (Chicago: GIA Publications, 2002), www.umcdiscipleship. org/resources/history-of-hymns-when-memory-fades.

9 781501 880247